ART SCHOOL CONFIDENTIAL

Official unexpurgated top-secret final
last-minute shooting draft by D. Clowes

SCHOOL PLAYGROUND
We see from our hero's point of view as he is methodically pummelled by two eleven-year-old bullies. Adolescent fists punch us in the face, a series of painful thuds. We switch angles to reveal **JEROME PLATZ**, *also eleven, who accepts the beating without resistance.*

SCHOOL CAFETERIA
Later that day, Jerome, slightly bruised, sits alone drawing in his math book. The bullies sit at a nearby table with some other bullies. We see Jerome's drawing: The two bullies are buried waist-deep in mud, screaming, while an idealized Jerome empties the contents of a gigantic toilet onto their heads. An overweight classmate looks over Jerome's shoulder and starts to giggle. Other kids gather around. One of the bullies notices all the commotion.

SCHOOL PLAYGROUND
We see Jerome being pounded, exactly as before. The camera moves up and away, drifting from the action. Over this, we hear:

JEROME (V.O.): I am a genius. I am the greatest artist of the twentieth century.

SCHOOL CLASSROOM

Jerome, dressed as Pablo Picasso (with rubber bald-wig and artist's palette), speaks to the class.

JEROME: I pretty much invented Modern Art, and I do weird abstract paintings even though I could paint totally realistic if I wanted to.

Everyone in the class wears a costume (Lincoln, a hockey player, Jesus).

JEROME (CONT'D): Also, even though I am super short and bald, I am able to have sex with any beautiful woman I want just because I'm so great.

Several students look back at the teacher, who tries to hide her discomfort with an inane grin.

SIX YEARS LATER

SCHOOL CAFETERIA
Close-up on a drawing, in progress, of a very **CUTE GIRL.**
*The camera tilts to reveal a perky seventeen-year-old, not
quite as cute as the drawing, facing us from across the
table. Jerome, also seventeen, finishes with a flourish and
presents it to her.*

CUTE GIRL: Wow!

To Jerome's disappointment, she beckons for her
BOYFRIEND.

BOYFRIEND: Pretty good.

CUTE GIRL: Someday if you get famous, this might
be worth a lot of money!

*The Boyfriend drags her away, leaving Jerome alone with
his nerdish friend,* **EUGENE.**

EUGENE: You're wasting your time, Jerome—you need
to set your sights on a more realistic girl.

JEROME: *(plaintively watching the Cute Girl recede into the distance)* I just need to get out of here and become a famous artist and everything else will fall into place.

Just then, **STOOB***, a lanky jock, grabs Jerome from behind and wrestles him out of his chair with a playful half-nelson.*

STOOB: Hey, Pencil-Prick—thanks for helping me out with that poster for Erikson's class. He said I was a natural artist!

JEROME: A natural scam artist.

STOOB: You got that right, queer-bait!

Stoob grabs something from Jerome's back pocket.

STOOB (CONT'D): Whaddayou, jackin' off in school now?

JEROME: *(trying in vain to get it back)* It's a college brochure, you moron!

STOOB: "Strathmore Institute." What the hell kind of college has a naked chick for a teacher?

JEROME: She's an art model, you stupid ape.

Stoob drops Jerome. He hands back the brochure with a conspiratorial grin.

STOOB: You're alright, Platz.

Stoob leaves to rejoin the in-crowd. Eugene takes the brochure and looks at the cover: A semi-nude model poses for a serious-looking professor and his class.

EUGENE: I don't know, Jerome...are you sure about this?

JEROME: I know what I'm doing.

EUGENE: It just seems a little too good to be true, don't you think?

He opens the brochure to a big, impressive photo of the picturesque Strathmore campus.

ART SCHOOL CAMPUS

The brochure photo dissolves to a static "live" image of the campus. The camera starts to move, revealing this to be the only presentable section of a graffiti-covered urban wasteland. We continue in the same direction toward the Strathmore Institute dorm (on which a banner reads: "Welcome Freshmen"), and on through a series of shots over which the main titles are superimposed:

A sobbing multi-pierced freshman hugs a filthy stuffed Panda as she waves goodbye to her parents.

Another kid drops his travel bag, spilling an array of elaborate drug paraphernalia.

A super-square suburban dad kisses his ridiculously-filthy homeless-looking daughter on the cheek.

A barefoot hippie girl winces in pain as she steps on broken glass.

And finally, the camera stops on our hero Jerome, as he waves to a departing Volvo and turns, with suitcase in hand, to face the dorm.

DORM ROOM

Jerome is unpacking his suitcase in a tiny dorm room. We meet his roommates: **VINCE***, a would-be tough-guy, and* **MATTHEW***, a WASPy, closet-case fashion major.*

6

Vince barks into his cell-phone head-set, away from the other two.

VINCE: Yeah, it's based on the whole thing with the campus murderer, but...HELL no, it ain't no boring-ass documentary—forget that shit!...Fuckin' A! Of COURSE there's gonna be TONS of action, are you kidding me?

MATTHEW: *(eyes easel, etc.)* You're an art major?

JEROME: Yeah, drawing and painting. What are you guys?

MATTHEW: I'm fashion; he's film, I guess.

VINCE: *(in background)* Are you for real!? You're shitting me, right?

MATTHEW: God, this is so depressing.

JEROME: What's wrong?

MATTHEW: Nothing, I just really, really miss my girl-friend.

VINCE: One hundred percent…You won't be sorry! I love you too, Grandpa! *(Hangs up)* YES!

A pause. He notices Jerome and Matthew.

VINCE (CONT'D): *(Extends hand)* I'm Vince.

JEROME: Jerome.

VINCE: What was your name again?

MATTHEW: Matthew.

VINCE: God, I'm so fucking jazzed—I get to make my movie!! *(waits in vain for one of them to ask about it)* Yeah, it's like this total balls-out epic about all the crazy shit that's been going down in the 'hood, y'know?

MATTHEW: *(emotionless)* That's fantastic.

VINCE: You guys freshmen?

They nod.

MATTHEW: What are you, a sophomore?

VINCE: Junior. You guys listen to me and you'll do alright.

MATTHEW: Why do you still live in the dorm?

VINCE: A lot of juniors live in the dorm. What's wrong with that? *(brief pause)* Hey, it keeps me real.

CAFETERIA
Vince and Jerome sit in the crowded cafeteria at dinner hour. Jerome looks around—he spots a gawky nebbish holding court for three doting art-girls.

VINCE: That guy's some hot-shit sculpture major.

It's official—Jerome is in paradise.

JEROME: I've never seen so many beautiful girls.

Matthew joins Vince and Jerome with his tray.

VINCE: Pff! This is nothing; you should've seen last year's crop. Enrollment's way off since the murders.

JEROME: What murders?

VINCE: You're shittin' me, right?

MATTHEW: I heard about it. Somebody killed a guy right on campus, or whatever.

VINCE: Three people in the neighborhood since March. *(back to Jerome)* You gotta be fuckin' with me— you really don't know about the Strathmore Strangler? He killed a guy like ten days ago! What are you, from out-of-state?

JEROME: No, the suburbs.

VINCE: Then you have no excuse! What about Richard Natwick?

JEROME: Who's that?

VINCE: Jesus!

JEROME: I don't really follow the news.

VINCE: Okay, I'm gonna give you the story, but you gotta pay attention...This is a huge story! This is national news, man!

JEROME: Okay, okay. I'm listening.

VINCE: *(takes a breath)* Okay, so right after the first murder there's this guy named Richard Natwick, who's like a second year painting major, and he has a show at the student center...

STUDENT GALLERY
In a cramped gallery, we see **RICHARD**, *a wild-eyed young man, standing proudly among a group of paintings that say things like "MURDER = GLORY" and "KILL A COP FOR FUN." Two fairly obvious* **PLAINCLOTHES COPS** *enter the gallery and look around.*

VINCE (V.O.): The cops don't get that this guy is just some artsy schmuck and they start asking around...

ART SCHOOL CAMPUS
We see news video of a series of female students.

FEMALE STUDENT #1: Yeah, it wouldn't shock me at all. He really creeps me out.

FEMALE STUDENT #2: He's always talking about blood and spiders and all that shit. I'm like, dude, whatever it is, get over it.

FEMALE STUDENT #3: Yeah, I'm sure it's him. He just has a very negative quality. Like a rapist/child molester quality, you know?

ART SCHOOL CAMPUS
Four cops grab Natwick as he emerges from the dorm.

RICHARD: Get your hands off me, you filthy—

They slam him face-first into the wall and cuff him.

VINCE (V.O.): So then a couple of the professors start to freak out and before you know it, he's like a fuckin' martyr all of a sudden.

CAMPUS
A large group of students chants "Art is not a crime!"

VINCE (V.O.): And so of course it turns out he's completely innocent and the cops have to totally eat shit.

RANCH HOUSE
A tan, suburban **MOM** *and* **DAD** *stand in front of a ranch house.*

MOM NATWICK: *(thick, slow Florida drawl)* He was still down here with us when that gal got stabbed.

DAD NATWICK: Strangled.

JEROME: So what happened to him?

VINCE: He had his fifteen minutes of fame and then he got hurt real bad during some crazy-ass performance art thing.

STUDIO

We see Richard, tied to the wall, naked, with jumper cables attached to his nipples.

RICHARD: Okay, hit the juice!

VINCE: Anyway, you gotta read my script. It's all in there. It's totally huge!

Jerome spots a beautiful girl sitting alone. Something about her is strangely familiar.

VINCE (CONT'D): So what, you don't get the paper in the suburbs?

Jerome flips back through his sketchbook to a drawing of the nude model from the Strathmore brochure.

VINCE (CONT'D): *(glancing at the sketchbook)*
So you're a drawing major?

Jerome notices that this girl has a distinctive necklace, similar to one the model was wearing, but he can't quite make a positive ID. She leaves.

JEROME: Drawing and painting.

VINCE: That's awesome. I hear you guys get to see tons of naked vagina!

FIGURE DRAWING CLASS
Jerome waits anxiously for his first figure drawing class to start. Classmates file in. **PROFESSOR SANDIFORD,** *45-ish, enters, enthusiastically clapping his hands.*

PROFESSOR SANDIFORD: Let's go, Leslie—time to work your magic! Fifteen minute pose, people! Let's hit the floor running!

Jerome hones in on who he hopes is the model: A pouty blonde wearing what looks like a bathrobe. From behind a screen, however, comes **LESLIE**, *a craggy, rat-haired drug addict who doffs his filthy dashiki and takes the stage. Jerome, undaunted, begins to draw; a strong, confident line. We see a series of drawings of various poses, all slightly ridiculous but handled by Jerome with deft aplomb.*

PROFESSOR SANDIFORD (CONT'D): I don't have any great wisdom to impart to you people other than these four magic words: DON'T HAVE UNREALISTIC EXPECTATIONS! If you want to make money you should drop out right now and go to banking school, or to website school...anywhere but art school! Remember, only one out of a hundred of you will ever make a living as an artist!

Jerome unconsciously adopts a heroic painterly stance as he draws. We move in on his determined face.

JEROME (V.O.): I'll be that one!

We dolly past Jerome to the faces of the other students.

SHILO (V.O.): I'll be that one.

ARMY-JACKET (V.O.): I'll be that one.

ENO (V.O.): I'll be that one.

And so on, down the line. Their voice-overs overlap each other, building to a cacophonous din. A cell phone rings. Sandiford goes to his bag to answer it.

PROFESSOR SANDIFORD: Hello? Yes? Well, hello Lorenzo...Absolutely...Yes...

LESLIE: *(ridiculous and unexpected nasal Brooklyn accent)* Can I get a break, Sandy?

PROFESSOR SANDIFORD: *(covering phone)* That's a break, people! Take five! *(continues with call)* Yes, I'd love for you to see them...I feel as though I've really turned a corner with this latest series...

Most of the students go out in the hall to smoke. Leslie wanders over to a preppy-ish girl and makes small talk, his "thing" hanging at eye-level. Sandiford wanders around the room, perusing the drawings with little enthusiasm as he talks on the phone He stops behind Jerome and gives a nod of approval.

PROFESSOR SANDIFORD: *(exiting)* Yes, January would be great...No, I don't think I have anything on my plate...

Jerome remains in the classroom during the break. A scrawny, ghoulish wise-ass, **BARDO**, *sidles over. He examines his fellow students as they reenter the room.*

17

BARDO: Jesus, why are the people in these freshman classes exactly the same every year? There's the angry lesbian, the boring blowhard, the vegan holy-man...

Jerome giggles. In the background, another student, **KISS-ASS***, follows the Professor back into the room.*

KISS-ASS: Professor, I just wanted to tell you that I looked up some of your paintings on the internet, and I thought they were really terrific.

PROFESSOR SANDIFORD: *(sarcastic)* You get an A for the semester.

Behind them enters another student, a middle-aged housewife.

BARDO: And there we have "Kiss-Ass," and "Mom." You get at least one of each in every class. Mom's youngest just left the nest and she's ready to "explore her creative side."

MOM: *(in background, to Sandiford)* ...I feel like I'm finally about to ripen, artistically.

JEROME: *(somewhat amazed)* How do you know all this stuff?

BARDO: Because I'm a living cliché just like everybody else. I'm the guy who keeps dropping out and changing his major because he's afraid he really sucks at everything.

Jerome takes this in.

JEROME: So who am I?

BARDO: I'm not sure. I haven't figured you out yet.

Trailing behind the others, a distinctive young man re-enters the classroom. He looks more like a suburban jock than a Bohemian navel-gazer, and as such stands in sharp contrast to his uniformly non-conformist classmates.

BARDO (CONT'D): Jesus, who's the weirdo?

19

DARK AUDITORIUM

Cut to pitch black, over which we hear the measured allo-cutions of art history professor **SOPHIE HOFFENKAMP**.

SOPHIE (V.O.): What is art?

Ka-chunk. A slide projector clicks. More blackness.

SOPHIE (V.O.) (CONT'D): Is this art?

A slide of the MONA LISA fills the frame and is strained into focus.

SOPHIE (V.O.) (CONT'D): Or this?

The VENUS OF WILLENDORF.

SOPHIE (V.O.) (CONT'D): Or this?

A TOOTHBRUSH.

SOPHIE (V.O.) (CONT'D): For centuries, this was art.

A CARAVAGGIO.

SOPHIE (V.O.) (CONT'D): And later, this…

A ROTHKO.

SOPHIE (V.O.) (CONT'D): And now, after thousands of years of development, mankind has arrived at the pinnacle of artistic achievement.

A DEFLATED BLUE WEATHER BALLOON sags over the edges of a museum pedestal. The lights come on and we see Sophie (mid-40s, tastefully dressed with a super-dry, ironic manner).

SOPHIE (V.O.) (CONT'D): Just because something is "new" and "fresh," does that necessarily mean it has any value? The art world has always put a premium on youth, on finding "the latest thing." In fact, if any of you kids haven't signed on with a major gallery by the end of this semester, you should probably just hang yourselves.

We see that most of the students find this mildly amusing, except for Jerome, who copies her words into his notebook like it's a homework assignment.

ANOTHER CLASSROOM

*Jerome and Bardo mindlessly knead large wads of clay,
while* **PROFESSOR OKAMURA**, *50-ish, talks one-on-one
with Kiss-Ass.*

KISS-ASS: Professor, what is your attendance policy?

PROFESSOR OKAMURA: I d-o-n-t c-a-r-e if you come
to class or not.

*He writes "don't care" on the blackboard as he says the
words. Meanwhile, Jerome has unconsciously made a
vague "cock and balls" shape with his clay.*

PROFESSOR OKAMURA (CONT'D): *(noticing this)* Hey,
don't try to make anything—just get a feel for it.

Jerome, embarrassed, crushes it into a lump.

BARDO: Okay, let me see if I got this right: You're the
guy who never got laid in high school, so you decided
to come here to bone your way through an endless
line-up of art-skanks.

JEROME: Not exactly...I mean, I really do want to be an artist...a great artist...you know, if possible.

BARDO: Which will enable you to bone a line-up of art-skanks. So, why wait? Art school is like a pussy buffet.

JEROME: I don't want just any girl.

Bardo looks around for a micro-second. He spots a cute classmate with a Bettie Page hair-do.

BARDO: Look, there she is, the beautiful beatnik art-chick of your dreams.

JEROME: Yeah, so?

BARDO: So go ask to borrow something. It's the easiest thing in the world.

Jerome hesitates; Bardo pushes him forward.

JEROME: Hi...Uh...could I...do you think I could borrow your pencil?

BEAT GIRL: Why? What for?

He can't think of a good reason.

JEROME: Oh, never m—

BEAT GIRL: Oh my God.

She grabs his arms and stares directly into his face.

BEAT GIRL (CONT'D): You have the most beautiful eyes. You have to let me take a picture of your eyes.

Jerome looks back at Bardo. It's a go-project.

BEAT GIRL'S DORM ROOM
The Beat Girl is curled up in a ball on the floor, laughing maniacally. Jerome reaches over to try to calm her down, but this elicits only an agonized wail.

JEROME: How about pizza? Do you want to go get pizza?

The maniacal laughter resumes.

CAMPUS

The class sits outside drawing a big rock. Bardo speaks as though continuing his thought from the previous scene.

BARDO: The only trouble is, all those beatnik chicks are totally insane. What you really want to find is a nice, innocent suburban girl—some freshman chick who hasn't been corrupted yet...

We pan past Jerome to reveal such a girl. She looks up from her drawing and smiles sweetly.

SUBURBAN GIRL'S APARTMENT

Jerome and **SUBURBAN GIRL** *are sitting on her canopy bed. Her room is decorated like a little girl's room ca. 1980. She is playing intently with her stuffed animals, completely oblivious to Jerome.*

SUBURBAN GIRL: *(little kid voice)* Stay out of that cave, Koala Bear—there's snakes and bats!

(gruff Koala bear voice) Don't be silly, Pepper. I'm not afraid of a little snake!

JEROME: Or if you don't want to do that, maybe we could go see a movie?

She ignores him.

SUBURBAN GIRL: *(as Koala Bear)* Well, look who's here—it's Doctor and Mrs. Walrus, on their way to Pillow-town.

SCHOOL STUDIO
Jerome and Bardo spray fixative on their finished drawings of the rock.

BARDO: Come to think of it, they're all insane. You should just find yourself some nympho slut and get it over with.

Again, the camera wastes no time in finding a specimen of this genus. She bites her lip seductively.

NYMPHO'S APARTMENT

The place is a filthy pig-sty, decorated with horrible paint-ings. Jerome sits next to her on the couch, leaning in to make his move. She stops him.

NYMPHO: Oh wait—I just want to tell you that I defi-nitely don't have AIDS. I've been tested like forty times, so I know it for a fact.

With that out of the way, she awaits the continuation of Jerome's advance. We hear a baby crying in the next room.

NYMPHO (CONT'D): *(shouting right next to Jerome's ear)* KEEP THE FUCKING KID QUIET, YOU MOTHER-FUCKING ASSHOLE!! *(back to Jerome)* It's just my old man.

DORM ROOM

Vince, Matthew and Jerome sit at their desks working. Jerome puts the finishing touches on his rock drawing. Matthew pins fabric to a dress-maker's dummy.

VINCE: Are you serious? You never been laid before?

JEROME: It just hasn't worked out. I have very high standards.

VINCE: Man, I gotta take you out whore-busting some night. We gotta remedy this situation before it gets any worse!

MATTHEW: *(projecting)* Maybe you have psychological issues that make it difficult for you to feel comfortable with your own sexuality.

As he speaks, he unconsciously jabs pins into the mannequin's crotch.

JEROME: Could be, I guess.

VINCE: You guys know what whore-busting is?

They don't bother to respond. Jerome stares out the window.

VINCE (CONT'D): That's when you leave the money on the dresser and you fuck the whore and go to sleep, and when you wake up in the morning not only is your money still there but she's left you a tip!

Jerome watches a girl walk past the dorm. Maybe he's hallucinating, but it looks once again like his dream girl from the brochure.

SCHOOL STUDIO
We dolly past a row of as-yet undecorated student work-space cubicles, to find Sandiford and his class assembled in front of a display wall covered with drawings of the big rock.

PROFESSOR SANDIFORD: *(going through the motions)* Does anybody see anything they like?

ENO: *(points)* That one has a certain particular tension that really seems to work.

KISS-ASS: It has a very palpable "rock-ness" to it.

PROFESSOR SANDIFORD: *(sighs)* What I find interesting is that none of you deviated from the parameters of the assignment. My rules are purely arbitrary, people —I expect you to come up with your own standards. God forbid you should try to second-guess what I'm looking for.

Jerome focuses on his own drawing which we see from his POV. The voices of the class fade down and give way to a triumphant Wagnerian chorus. The drawing remains in place as a new background dissolves in—it is now in a gilt-edged frame, behind a red velvet rope. The music swells. We dolly right; the next painting is a Michelangelo.

DARK AUDITORIUM

We hold on the Michelangelo. The music is replaced by the restless murmur of the art history class. The slide projector clicks through a series of 16th-century master paintings.

SOPHIE: If you are seeing these for the first time, feel free to weep with joy.

She continues clicking. Among the images, surprisingly, is a snapshot of a younger Sophie standing with a grim-faced bearded man on an undefined European bridge. She clicks past it expeditiously.

GIRL #2: Who was that?

SOPHIE: Ignore that. It was just a mistake.

She clicks until the screen goes black and then turns up the lights.

SOPHIE (CONT'D): Hamlet, War and Peace, Beethoven's Ninth, Guernica…These are works which hold as much emotional resonance today as they did in the time of their creation. What makes a work of art timeless? What qualities must it possess?

We see that Jerome is paying close attention. He writes down "Hamlet, War and Peace, etc" in his notebook.

SOPHIE (CONT'D): *(spots girl with her hand up)* Yes?

GIRL #1: Everything on your list was done by a dead white male.

GIRL #2: Yeah, I noticed that, too.

SOPHIE: *(deadpan)* Well, to be clear, they were not yet dead when they created those works.

GIRL #1: You're just playing into the hands of the patriarchy.

Jerome waits patiently for the lecture to continue.

ENO: Let's face it, the history of art is largely about the implementation of masculinity.

GIRL #1: Oh, that is such bullshit...

ENO: It's all part of some Darwinian imperative. Most artists become artists because they have no other way to attract a mate. Take a look—I hardly think I'm the first to point out that a vast preponderance of artists are, shall we say, physiologically deficient in some way.

GYMNASIUM
A co-ed basketball game is in progress. A bull-dyke drives to the hoop for an uncontested lay-up. Kiss-Ass gets the ball and lazily tosses it to an obese teammate, **HURST**, *who carries it at arm's length down the court.*

COACH: DRIBBLE, Hurst!

HURST: *(shaken)* Please don't yell.

We find Jerome warming the bench next to two cute art-school **COEDS.** *They are doing their nails, oblivious to the game.*

COED#1: Are you going to the Marvin Bushmiller talk tonight?

COED#2: Yeah, are you?

COED#1: Yeah, but we better get there early.

COED#2: It's weird how he's so famous and everything. I used to see him around Strathmore all the time when I was a freshman.

COED#1: I remember going to his show at Broadway Bob's, and then the next thing I know he's on the cover of *ARTFORUM.*

COED#2: Yeah, well, that's how it works.

COACH: *(blowing his whistle)* PLATZ! Get in there!

Jerome is given the ball. He tries to dribble, but it is immediately stolen by an aggressive tattooed guy, who passes the ball to a very effeminate teammate. It glances off his head and he bursts immediately into tears.

COACH (CONT'D): I gotta go back to teaching retards.

AUDITORIUM
MARVIN BUSHMILLER, *25, is on stage seated next to* **DAVID ZIPKIN**, *a sycophantic, James Lipton-ish professor. In the audience we see Jerome, sitting next to his classmate, Army-Jacket.*

QUESTIONER #1: The *New York Times* has called your work "an expedition to the far contours of an evolving techno-culture." With that in mind, where do you see art headed in the 21st century?

PROFESSOR ZIPKIN: Now there's an easy one!
(mild laughter from the audience)

MARVIN BUSHMILLER: Art who? *(more laughter)* No really, that's such a stupid question. Why don't you ask me something relevant? Ask me how much money

I have in the bank...

QUESTIONER #2: Did you learn anything at Strathmore? *(mild laughter builds to a smattering of applause)*

MARVIN BUSHMILLER: Yes, I learned many things: I learned that the faculty is made up of old failures who teach only because they need the health insurance. Present company excluded, of course.

PROFESSOR ZIPKIN: I was about to say...
(embarrassed laughter)

MARVIN BUSHMILLER: No, David here was too busy trolling the halls for fresh meat to worry about his health. *(More pained laughter)*

QUESTIONER #1: What advice would you give to a—

MARVIN BUSHMILLER: Look, there's really only one question any of you want to ask: You want to know what it would take to turn you into me. Now listen closely, because I'm going to give you the answer: In order to be a great artist you simply have to be a great artist. There's nothing to learn, so you're all wasting your time. Go home.

Army-Jacket raises his hand.

ARMY-JACKET: Why are you such an asshole?

The audience murmurs. Jerome leans as far away from A-J as possible.

MARVIN BUSHMILLER: That's a great question! *(relieved laughter from the audience)* No, really. It really is. I am an asshole because it is my true nature. Maybe it's everybody's true nature. Every single one of you looks like a fucking asshole to me, but who knows? The difference between you and me is that I have gained the freedom to express my true nature. And what could be more beautiful than truth and freedom?

The audience applauds enthusiastically, Jerome clapping loudest of all.

SANDIFORD'S CUBICLE

Professor Okamura enters to refill his coffee cup from a communal pot. Sandiford sits, flipping through his address book.

PROFESSOR OKAMURA: *(joyless, perfunctory)* Another day, another dollar.

PROFESSOR SANDIFORD: *(unenthusiastic)* Morning, Larry.

Okamura adds non-dairy creamer to his coffee.

PROFESSOR SANDIFORD (CONT'D): Tell me, Larry— do you and Lois have any plans for the evening of January the 18th?

PROFESSOR OKAMURA: How the hell should I know?

PROFESSOR SANDIFORD: It's just that I'm having a little gallery thing...Lorenzo Massengill wants to show some of my new paintings at his new space and I wanted to be sure to add your names to the invitation list.

PROFESSOR OKAMURA: I think I'm busy that night, Sandiford.

FIGURE DRAWING CLASS
Bardo enters.

BARDO: *(hands Jerome a cup of take-out coffee)* Here. I stopped off at Broadway Bob's.

JEROME: What is Broadway Bob's, anyway? I thought it was like a gallery, or something.

BARDO: It's a very famous shithole run by an obnoxious windbag who takes credit for launching the career of every half-talented monkey who ever took a class at Strathmore...but the coffee's pretty good.

Bardo slurps his coffee. We see Sandiford at his desk as he leaves a message on his cell phone.

PROFESSOR SANDIFORD: Hello, Lorenzo, I just wanted to make sure you received the slides...no need to call me back...

Suddenly we hear the clacking of heels and an out-of-breath female voice.

AUDREY: Sorry I'm late!

Into the room bursts **AUDREY**, *the girl from the cafeteria! His dream girl from the brochure! She stomps across the floor and disappears behind the screen.*

BARDO: *(out of the side of his mouth)* Looks like this is our lucky day.

She emerges in a terry-cloth bathrobe and takes the stage. She gracefully sheds the robe and assumes a standing pose. She is wearing nothing but the distinctive necklace, which Jerome sees clearly for the first time. He is absolutely overwhelmed. He begins to draw very carefully, angrily erasing the first few imperfect lines. We see the drawing develop in a series of time-lapse intercuts. Suddenly, she breaks the pose.

AUDREY: I'm sorry Sandy, I'm just dying for a cigarette.

PROFESSOR SANDIFORD: That's a break, people!

She puts on her robe and skips out into the hall. Jerome watches her leave. Bardo pretends to reach for Jerome's drawing.

BARDO: I'm going to the john—let me borrow this.

Jerome swats him away. Exit Bardo. Jerome continues to work on the drawing. Audrey reenters, and wanders toward Jerome's easel. His heart is pounding out of control as she carefully scrutinizes his work.

AUDREY: You really captured my otherness.

He smiles, not exactly sure whether this is good or bad.

BAD NEIGHBORHOOD
Jerome and Bardo walk briskly through the horrible neighborhood beyond the gates of the campus. **SCARY LOCALS** *taunt them.*

SCARY LOCAL #1: Hey faggots!

SCARY LOCAL #2: What a cute couple!

They ignore them as best they can. Jerome is still thinking about that model.

JEROME: So you've seen her before? Who is she?

BARDO: Don't get your hopes up. That's prime real estate, my friend.

JEROME: Is she a student, or just a model? Do you—

BARDO: *(interrupts)* Look, forget about her for one minute—you're about to have a life-changing experience!

SCARY LOCAL #1: Why don't you paint me a pretty picture, fag-boy?

JIMMY'S VESTIBULE
Bardo presses a rusty buzzer. After a long wait, there is a burst of static but no response.

BARDO: Hey Jimmy, it's Bardo. I brought someone over to meet you.

Another crackly pause.

BARDO (CONT'D): I've got a bottle of Slivovitz for you. *(Reads label)* It's 80 proof, made in Poland, imported by the—

BZZZZT.

JIMMY'S APARTMENT

JIMMY, *middle-aged, opens the door with a disarming cheerfulness. He looks friendly and avuncular, like a dishevelled newscaster.*

JIMMY: Boys, welcome! I'm afraid you caught me in the middle of one of my shows.

We enter the living room. Like Jimmy, it all looks pleasant enough on the surface, but as we get closer we see just how shabby and drab and run-down everything is. The theme song to The Facts of Life *drones from a TV in the back room.*

BARDO: This is Jerome.

JIMMY: A pleasure.

Jimmy clenches Jerome's hand and makes meaningful eye-contact with him for an uncomfortable moment. They sit.

BARDO: Isn't this a great place? Jimmy's got rent control.

Jerome smiles and nods politely. Jimmy selects a large, filthy paper cup from the wastebasket and casually fills it to the top with Slivovitz.

BARDO (CONT'D): *(with evil smirk)* Jerome here wants to be a great artist, Jimmy.

JIMMY: How terrific.

Jerome makes a self-deprecating, "aw shucks" gesture.

JIMMY (CONT'D): Tell me, Jerome, are you exceptionally skilled as a cock-sucker?

Jerome laughs and averts eye-contact. There is an uncomfortable pause.

JIMMY (CONT'D): That wasn't a rhetorical question, Jerome. Are you a "great artist" when it comes to fellatio?

JEROME: No, I guess not.

JIMMY: That's no good.

He takes two big gulps.

JIMMY (CONT'D): So who do you like?

JEROME: Hmm?

JIMMY: "Hmm?" Who is your favorite artist, Jerome?

JEROME: *(takes his time trying to come up with a safe answer)* Maybe Picasso.

JIMMY: Oh, I see. Very good. Our old friend Pick-ass-hole: The nasty little dwarf who went his whole life without a single original thought. I presume you're joking?

He takes another hearty slug.

BARDO: Jimmy's a Strathmore grad.

JIMMY: *(with mock pride)* And just look at me now!

He looks around at his squalid furnishings.

JIMMY (CONT'D): Just think, Jerome, one day this could all be yours! You're going places, young man, I can feel it!

Jerome laughs politely, but Jimmy isn't done yet.

JIMMY (CONT'D): But you really need to take some lessons in cock-sucking and ass-licking! Otherwise, you might find yourself rotting away in some shithole, postponing suicide for the slim chance that you might possibly one day see some glorious plague or pesti-lence bring horrible suffering to your hateful species! *(to Jerome)* What are you smiling about??!

Jerome can't seem to wipe the silly smirk off his face.

JIMMY (CONT'D): Laugh away, laughing boy!! I will stomp your guts till they shoot out your ass!! I will bury you alive and shit on your grave!!

He pours the last ounce from the bottle and slugs it down. He glances back at the TV in the other room, on which we see a blurry Mindy Cohn.

JIMMY (CONT'D): Okay boys, show's over. I have to get back to my masturbation.

He shoos them out.

BAD NEIGHBORHOOD
They walk home along the same street.

BARDO: Isn't Jimmy great?

JEROME: Definitely.

FIGURE DRAWING CLASS
Professor Sandiford stands in front of a wall of self-portraits. Jerome's is by far the most impressive.

PROFESSOR SANDIFORD: Starting next week, I will be selecting the most effective piece from each session and placing it in the hall gallery with the best work from some of the other classes.

VEGAN: Which gallery?

PROFESSOR SANDIFORD: On this floor, down at the end of the hall.

ARMY-JACKET: *(incredulous)* By the men's toilet?

PROFESSOR SANDIFORD: *(somewhat exasperated)* Yes. *(turns to the self-portraits)* All right, let's get going on these. Who wants to start?

Jerome straightens up. A **FILTHY-HAIRED GIRL** *points to a crude abstract doodle.*

FILTHY-HAIRED GIRL: I like Flower's drawing.

SHILO: Yeah, me too.

ENO: It seems like she's trying to do something more than just draw herself. It's really more about the process of drawing.

Jerome looks at Bardo—are they serious?

PROFESSOR SANDIFORD: Is there anything else up here that commands your attention?

Again, Jerome straightens. No response.

PROFESSOR SANDIFORD (CONT'D): Anything more on Flower's piece?

Jerome sighs.

PROFESSOR SANDIFORD (CONT'D): Yes, Jerome?

JEROME: Nothing.

PROFESSOR SANDIFORD: There's no such thing as nothing in this class. Tell us what you think.

Jerome holds his tongue.

PROFESSOR SANDIFORD (CONT'D): We're waiting, Jerome.

JEROME: I don't know...I mean, it's just a lame Cy Twombly imitation and it looks like she did it in about two minutes.

The class is shocked. Flower bursts into tears.

FILTHY-HAIRED GIRL: That is such bullshit! Just because her drawing isn't perfect, you act like it's automatically bad!

SHILO: Yeah, at least it has humanity!

VEGAN: Yeah, totally! Jerome's drawing looks like it was done by a machine! Flower's is full of playfulness and...and yeah, like, humanity.

JEROME: *(defensively coopting Jimmy's shtick)* What's so great about humanity? Humans are a bunch of jerks! I hope some plague wipes out the whole species!

The class erupts; Jerome is berated from all sides. Bardo finds the whole thing highly amusing.

PROFESSOR SANDIFORD: Okay, people, that's enough. I am required to give you these kinds of assignments, but they are CERTAINLY nothing to CRY about, Flower. Now I want everybody to kiss and make up because we will soon be moving on to far more important stuff.

FIGURE DRAWING CLASS—LATER
Jerome, angry and regretful, is packing up his stuff.
JONAH, *the overly-normal jock, approaches.*

JONAH: Man, I agree with you one hundred percent.

JEROME: Huh?

JONAH: I think the entire human race should be wiped off the face of the earth.

JEROME: Oh, I didn't really...I mean, I was just—you know...

JONAH: Hey, you don't have to apologize. I'm totally with you.

HALLWAY
Jerome and Bardo round a corner to inspect the Hall Gallery, which is really nothing more than a dingy, water-stained bulletin board. A construction-paper sign reads "Strathmore's Finest."

BARDO: Jesus, that's sad.

Two **BAKED SOPHOMORES** *exit the adjacent men's room making fart noises and giggling. Jerome looks at the empty bulletin board with nothing less than reverence and awe. SHILO approaches them.*

SHILO: Hey, you guys have to come to my opening tonight.

She gives each of them a flyer.

SHILO (CONT'D): *(To Jerome)* You were really an asshole in class today.

She exits to chase after the Baked Sophomores.

BARDO: Don't you want to see Shilo's "opening"?

He makes a vagina shape with his fingers.

JEROME: How did she ever get a gallery show?

BARDO: It's totally meaningless. Any idiot can sign up for one of those student galleries.

They each look at the flyer, a grainy Xerox with several of Shilo's black-and-white photos. One of them catches Jerome's eye—it looks like Audrey!

BARDO (CONT'D): Oh man, I didn't notice that! We gotta go!

Bardo points to the line at the bottom of the flyer that reads "FREE REFRESHMENTS."

STUDENT GALLERY
It's a group show with no cohesive theme (a few sculptures, some small collages, and Shilo's photos). All ten or so attendees surround a central food/beer table with their backs to the art. Jonah is there, keeping to himself.

BARDO: *(Mouth full, scanning the table for more food)* Great work, Shilo.

Only Jerome looks at the art, specifically the photo of Audrey. Shilo wanders over.

JEROME: Do you know this girl?

SHILO: We had her as a model, remember?

JEROME: Do you know who she is? Do you know her name?

SHILO: God, you're such a prick. Can't you say anything nice about my pictures?

Suddenly, a voice comes from behind them.

AUDREY: Hi.

Jerome whips around. Audrey steps up to the portrait.

AUDREY (CONT'D): Oh wow, that came out really good.

She's clearly just being nice, but the gesture is somehow very sweet. She recognizes Jerome.

AUDREY (CONT'D): Oh, hi.

Bardo approaches. Audrey looks at another picture, then turns back to Jerome.

AUDREY (CONT'D): I'm Audrey, by the way.

BARDO: *(cutting in)* Is that your real name, or are you just obsessed with Audrey Hepburn like every other art school chick?

AUDREY: Actually, I was named after an old cartoon.

She fishes a LITTLE AUDREY necklace from inside her shirt.

BARDO: Oh wow, an ironic pop-culture reference.

Jerome glares at him. Audrey starts to edge away. Just then, the Baked Sophomores enter with a case of beer. Bardo makes a beeline for the table.

JEROME: Do you know that guy?

AUDREY: No, I thought he was your friend.

JEROME: No way.

AUDREY: Oh, you're the guy from Sandy's class. I have such a bad memory for faces. I'm sorry.

JEROME: It's okay. I'm Jerome.

AUDREY: I was just thinking about you today. I saw an old photo of Marie-Therese Walter that looked just like the way you drew me.

Jerome's eyes glaze over in a lovesick stupor.

AUDREY (CONT'D): She's one of the women who modeled for Picasso.

JEROME: *(snaps out of it)* I know who she is. I know just the picture you're talking about.

AUDREY: You do?

Jerome notices that Bardo is headed back toward them, holding two beers.

JEROME: *(gallantly)* Uh-oh, let's get out of here!

He guides her through the crowd out into the hall, losing Bardo, whom we see in the background being cornered by Shilo.

AUDREY: You didn't have to do that.

JEROME: I couldn't bear to watch you get cornered by that creep again.

AUDREY: I have to get going, anyway. I'm kind of making the rounds tonight.

JEROME: *(disappointed)* Oh really? Well, maybe some time we could—

AUDREY: I have to go to a Donald Baumgarten show.

JEROME: Oh, I've heard of him. He's an old pop art guy, right? Yeah, he's really good...he's great.

AUDREY: He's absolutely awful, but I can't get out of it. *(a pause, then suddenly)* Do you want to go with me?

Jerome is dumbstruck.

AUDREY (CONT'D): C'mon, please? I hate to take the subway by myself, especially with that weirdo out there strangling everybody.

SUBWAY TRAIN

Jerome and Audrey try to talk, but can't hear each other over the noise of the train. Jerome looks at their reflection in the window. What a cute couple! Romantic music over-takes the subway noise. He moves his hand slightly closer to hers.

GALLERY

They enter the gallery. Audrey is radiant and graceful as she makes her way through the crowd. Everyone seems to know her. Jerome hovers a step behind, soaking it all in. We wind up in the back of the gallery where a weather-beaten grey-haired, pony-tailed artiste sits among others of his ilk.

AUDREY: Hi.

The pony-tailed man turns around. His craggy face betrays a life of hardship, alcoholism, etc.

DONALD BAUMGARTEN: Audrey! I was afraid you weren't coming!

He hugs her.

AUDREY: So how's it going?

DONALD BAUMGARTEN: I think I might have sold two of the small ones...the ones you hate.

AUDREY: I like them just fine, you know that...just not as much as the big, blue ones.

DONALD BAUMGARTEN: I know...

AUDREY: Daddy, this is Jerome. He's a big fan of yours, so I brought him here to meet you. Jerome, this is Donald Baumgarten.

Jerome's jaw practically hits the floor. This is her father? He gives Audrey a "why didn't you tell me?" look.

JEROME: Wow, it's a real honor to meet you, sir.

DONALD BAUMGARTEN: My pleasure, son.

AUDREY: I hate to do this, Daddy, but we're going to have to leave in a minute.

DONALD BAUMGARTEN: But you just got here.

AUDREY: I know, but Jerome has to meet someone at another party and we're already late.

Jerome is a bit startled by this but nods along.

DONALD BAUMGARTEN: Well, thank you for coming, sugar...will I see you Sunday?

AUDREY: I'll call you. Congratulations!

STREET
They exit. Audrey, relieved, stops to light a cigarette.

AUDREY: Well, I did my good deed for the week.

They head for the subway entrance.

JEROME: I can't believe you grew up with a dad like that...I mean, he's a famous artist!

AUDREY: He's hardly a famous artist. Really, it's just embarrassing. He should have given up thirty years ago. *(a pause)* God, I'm starving.

BROADWAY BOB'S COFFEE HOUSE

Our couple sits, eating dessert in this legendary art-world hang-out. Jerome spots a distinguished-looking grey-haired man drawing in his sketchbook while his date looks on.

JEROME: Is that who I think it is?

AUDREY: He's always here. That table is practically reserved for Post-minimalists.

Jerome looks around, taking it all in.

AUDREY (CONT'D): This is where everybody gets their first big show. It's like the launching pad from Strathmore to the real world.

JEROME: *(with false nonchalance)* So how do they pick who gets a show?

AUDREY: Oh, you know...they go to the surveys and all that...

BROADWAY BOB *appears at their table.*

BROADWAY BOB: What's the matter? Don't you love me anymore? When's the last time you came to see me?

Audrey stands up and kisses him, as one would a favorite uncle.

AUDREY: Jerome, this is Broadway Bob.

Bob half-heartedly extends his hand without ever once glancing in Jerome's direction.

BROADWAY BOB: Yeah, how ya doin'?

AUDREY: Bob knows everybody.

BROADWAY BOB: Every artist you can think of had their first show in this place—Bushmiller, Naugle, Bilbo—you name it. And the minute they get famous they got no time for me!

He spots something across the room.

BROADWAY BOB (CONT'D): *(yelling)* Hey! I told you to stop hassling my customers! Hector!

A plain-clothes detective and a uniformed officer are talking to a table of art students. **HECTOR**, *Bob's assistant, emerges from the back and heads for the cops.*

BROADWAY BOB (CONT'D): Fucking brown-shirts! *(To Audrey, as he stomps off)* Good to see you, sweetheart. Say hi to your father.

They watch from across the room as Bob and Hector usher the cops toward the door. From behind Jerome, a sinewy, Patti-Smithish 24-year-old, **CANDACE,** *appears. She seems to be well-acquainted with Audrey.*

CANDACE: *(pointing at Jerome)* Who's this?

AUDREY: *(not too happy to see her)* Jerome. Jerome, this is Candace.

Jerome extends his hand. Candace stares at it.

CANDACE: Audrey and I used to bump cunts.

Jerome is a little thrown.

CANDACE (CONT'D): *(with flat insincerity)* Just kidding. Ha ha. *(she stares at Audrey)* But little Audrey doesn't want to play with me anymore, does she? *(shifting back to Jerome)* What do you think of these paintings?

JEROME: They're fine...I mean they're not the most—you know...

AUDREY: They're Candace's paintings.

JEROME: Oh, I didn't mean—I mean, I think they're really good, I just—

CANDACE: Where DO you find them, Audrey? Anyway, thanks to this little exhibit it looks like I'm getting a spring show at the Haberman.

JEROME: Wow, that's really great—congratulations!

CANDACE: Golly gosh!!

She pinches his cheek. Broadway Bob beckons for her.

BROADWAY BOB: You! Get over here!

CANDACE: Later, kids.

She vanishes into Bob's office. Jerome notices for the first time the subject of the painting across from them.

JEROME: Is that you?

Audrey nods.

JEROME (CONT'D): It doesn't really capture you.

AUDREY: Nope.

JEROME: So why are you a model? Just for the money?

AUDREY: Oh yeah, I make a fortune.

JEROME: Are you paying your way through school?

AUDREY: That's what I used to say, but I dropped out a long time ago.

She thinks about it.

AUDREY (CONT'D): I guess I haven't figured out what else to do...I can't seem to tear myself away from this place...

Jerome focuses with great intensity on her every word.

JEROME: You know, nobody ever gives the model any credit, but in a way, they're just as important as the artist. It's really much more of a collaboration than people think.

She smiles, charmed by his apparent sincerity.

AUDREY: So, what do you want to do, Jerome?

Jerome tries his best to look dignified and confident. This is his big moment to sell himself.

JEROME: I want to be the greatest artist of the twenty-first century.

AUDREY: *(giggles)* I just meant what do you want to do now? I should probably get home.

JEROME: *(embarrassed)* Oh, jeez, I'm sorry, I...

AUDREY: No, I think that's great. I think you really could be a great artist. You have the right kind of energy.

He looks her directly in the eye. Did she really say what he thinks she said?

DORM ROOM
A buoyant Jerome enters. Vince, wearing only his underpants, types furiously at the computer.

JEROME: You won't believe what I—

VINCE: *(rudely interrupting)* Did you hear the news?

JEROME: No, but guess what I—

VINCE: The strangler got another one—some poor schmuck on his way to the subway. *(continues clacking away)* I got some major rewriting to do.

JEROME: Jesus, really? I was on the subway tonight.

VINCE: You're lucky to be alive.

JEROME: So guess what I was doing.

VINCE: Smoking pole?

JEROME: No, I was out on a date with the most beautiful girl in the whole school.

VINCE: Well alright...Can I smell your finger?

Jerome rummages through his stuff until he finds the old brochure.

JEROME: Look.

He points to her photo.

VINCE: *(stops typing)* No shit. Nice.

JEROME: She thinks I'm a great artist.

VINCE: You fuckin' snake! So what the fuck are you doin' here, man? Did you already pop her?

JEROME: No...I mean, we just met. I—

VINCE: Man, if she was my girlfriend I'd be poundin' that shit day and night!

CLASSROOM

Prof. Sandiford paces around the room as he talks, pausing to give an unwanted back-rub or two.

PROFESSOR SANDIFORD: *(speaking with carnival-barker gravity)* NOVEMBER TWENTY-SEVENTH! Keep this date in your drug-addled little brains! This will be the day of THE POST-THANKSGIVING ASSESSMENT, where each of you will put up all your work and a bunch of us professors will sneak in behind your backs and give you a grade.

He moves toward a big wall calendar. There is a red star in the middle of December.

PROFESSOR SANDIFORD (CONT'D): HOWEVER, it is but a mere prelude, a dress rehearsal, for THIS day.

His finger THUMPS into the red star.

PROFESSOR SANDIFORD (CONT'D): DECEMBER EIGHTEENTH. The FINAL SURVEY. Here, you will receive your one and only official grade for the class... provided, of course, you haven't all been murdered by then!

No one laughs at his little joke.

ARMY-JACKET: I heard that the final survey is where a lot of big-shot gallery owners and stuff show up to troll for new talent.

PROFESSOR SANDIFORD: *(bemused)* Well, I wouldn't worry about that too much.

ARMY-JACKET: All I'm saying is this could be a big break for somebody.

PROFESSOR SANDIFORD: This is not Schwab's drug store, young man, and you are definitely not Lana Turner.

ARMY-JACKET: *(taking it personally)* What does that mean?

PROFESSOR SANDIFORD: It means that you children are many, many years away from such worries. *(shifts gears)* Eno! Why haven't you been doing the assignments?

ENO: Frankly, I find them constricting, and largely irrelevant. My work has nothing to do with form or light or color, but with questioning the nature of aesthetic experience.

PROFESSOR SANDIFORD: I'll buy that. Jonah? How about you?

Jerome and Bardo perk up.

JONAH: I'll...uh...I'll bring something in next time... sorry.

ARMY-JACKET: I also heard that the student with the best grade in the final survey gets to have a one-man show at Broadway Bob's.

PROFESSOR SANDIFORD: That has been known to happen, yes.

ARMY-JACKET: Professor Okamura told me that no one from your class has ever gotten the best grade.

PROFESSOR SANDIFORD: *(irked)* Well, Larry tends to care about these things a lot more than I do...

ARMY-JACKET: I also heard they're cutting faculty next semester and all the profs are shitting bricks over getting a student to win the Broadway Bob show.

PROFESSOR SANDIFORD: I'm afraid I'm much too involved in my own painting to get caught up in any of the faculty intrigue.

FLOWER: Isn't it true that Marvin Bushmiller got his big break when he got the best grade in the survey?

The rest of the class joins in, barraging Professor Sandiford with questions. He slumps, defeated.

BROADWAY BOB'S COFFEE HOUSE

Jerome sits alone drinking coffee. He studies a photograph on the wall of Marvin Bushmiller shaking hands with Broadway Bob. Audrey enters. Jerome waves and joins her at the counter. She pours herself a cup of coffee.

AUDREY: I just came in to get a coffee. *(She glances at her watch)* I have to model for Professor Bogle's class at six-thirty.

JEROME: Can I walk with you?

AUDREY: God, you're so polite.

CAMPUS

They walk through the campus. The sun is just starting to set, giving the sky an otherworldly golden hue.

JEROME: So what are you doing this weekend?

AUDREY: I don't know...I never know until the last minute.

JEROME: Well, I was thinking maybe we—

VINCE (O.S.): *(shouting)* JEROME! WAIT UP YOU STUPID TWAT!

Vince runs up behind them with his video camera. Jerome is mortified. Any connection to a creep like Vince could kill his chances.

JEROME: This is—uh—my roommate...

He gives Audrey a "can you believe I'm stuck living with this guy?" look.

VINCE: *(sweating and out-of-breath)* This is perfect!

JEROME: Look, we have to go.

VINCE: This will only take a second. I need an insert shot of a couple kissing, and this light is awesomely perfect.

JEROME: *(pushing him away)* Look, we don't have time right now, okay. I'm sure you can find plenty—

AUDREY: Oh c'mon, I don't mind.

VINCE: Excellent! Follow me.

He leads them to a picturesque corner and positions them. Jerome is not quite ready for this.

VINCE (CONT'D): Okay, action! Go for it!

They kiss. It's the greatest moment of Jerome's life, whether his dream girl is merely acting or not.

VINCE (CONT'D): *(Lowers the camera)* Awesome work, people!

CLASSROOM

Jerome and Bardo mount their drawings to the wall. Bardo nudges Jerome and nods toward the door. Jonah enters, carrying a large canvas.

PROFESSOR SANDIFORD: From now on there are no official assignments. Last week I asked you to bring in what you thought was your best work, old or new. This will be the starting point from which some of you will, I hope, grow into artists.

He walks along the wall, pausing briefly at Army-Jacket's painting, which features a headline that reads "We live in a police state."

PROFESSOR SANDIFORD (CONT'D): Ain't that the truth?

He continues on down the line, toward Jerome's painting— a small color portrait of Audrey, based on the original figure drawing.

PROFESSOR SANDIFORD (CONT'D): Well, what have we here?

Jerome smiles. At last! But Sandiford skips right past and goes to the next piece, a ridiculous mess of wires, circuits, and christmas lights.

PROFESSOR SANDIFORD (CONT'D): *(after a two-second appraisal)* It'll never fly, Wilbur!

A mousey Asian girl slumps. Jerome watches in disbelief as Sandy continues on.

PROFESSOR SANDIFORD (CONT'D): Whose is this?

Bardo elbows Jerome.

JONAH: Oh, that's mine.

We see his painting—it's a big, bold, very simple picture of a sports car. The technique is seemingly crude, as though painted by a child, but it has a certain compelling purity. Sandy studies it for a very long time.

PROFESSOR SANDIFORD: Where have you been all my life?

Jonah chuckles uncomfortably.

PROFESSOR SANDIFORD (CONT'D): What does everyone think?

FLOWER: It's so...I mean, it's like he figured out how to unlearn all the typical art-school bullshit...it's really great!

ENO: It has the singularity of outsider art, though the conscious rejection of spatial dynamics could only come from an intimacy with the conventions of picture-making.

Jerome, slowly boiling, finally explodes.

JEROME: Are you kidding me? This is the absolute— I mean, how can you possibly...

The entire class glares at him.

JEROME (CONT'D): *(bitterly; it's not worth pursuing)* Forget it...

Professor Sandiford moves along to a goofy "drawing" done with what looks to be silly string.

PROFESSOR SANDIFORD: This is interesting...

ENO: It's not quite finished, but I thought the class might like to see the various stages of my process.

Jonah looks back and catches Jerome's steely glare. They eye each other like two gunfighters across the saloon.

SCHOOL EDITING ROOM

We see Vince, his bearded assistant **JASON***, and Jason's bored girlfriend,* **DONNA** *sitting in a dark editing room watching a small monitor.*

MONTAGE

On grainy video we see the following scenes of campus life:
Students playing frisbee.
An old professor feeding the pigeons.
A couple (Jerome and Audrey) kissing.
Over this we hear a sinister monologue:

STRANGLER (V.O.): Look at you—so content with your happy little lives! But none of you know the taste of true happiness...the happiness that only death can bring!

We see a dark figure from the back as he surveys the campus.

STRANGLER (CONT'D): I am hell on earth personified!

He pulls a small rope taut with his gloved hands, holding it awkwardly to the side so that it can be seen on camera from behind.

CAMPUS

The video continues: The camera moves with annoying self-consciousness, as loud rap music blares. Leslie, the craggy male art-model, playing a tough-but-honest police detective, brutally interrogates a low-life street-informant played by Hurst (the chubby kid from gym class).

LESLIE: *(trying, and failing miserably, to sound "tough")* Listen, dick-sucker—if I find out you know something, I'm gonna turn your face into ground mother-fucking round—understand?

HURST: *(trying/failing to sound "street")* I–I swear I don't know nothing about no murders, man!

LESLIE: If another corpse turns up on my beat, I will hold you personally responsible!

He slaps him hard across the face. Hurst moans. We hold on his uncomfortable grimace far too long before the screen goes black.

SCHOOL EDITING ROOM

Vince turns on the lights. Jason sits at an editing station by the monitor.

JASON: Whaddya think? Should I trim that last part?

Donna gets up to leave.

DONNA: *(to Jason)* How much longer are you gonna be?

JASON: It's up to the boss.

He nods at Vince, who scowls back at him. Donna kisses Jason and heads for the door.

VINCE: Hey, hey, hey! You can't just leave! What do you think of the movie so far?

DONNA: *(completely blank-faced)* It's fine.

VINCE: *(glaring)* Yeah, thanks.

She leaves. Vince stews for a minute.

JASON: She doesn't really get this kinda shit, y'know? I wouldn't worry about it.

VINCE: I gotta cram some kind of love story into this thing. Skags make up fifty percent of the audience!

HALLWAY
Jerome, on his way to class, runs into Kiss-Ass.

KISS-ASS: *(excited)* They're putting up the work in the hall gallery for the first time!

Jerome goes to investigate. There is a small crowd gathered at the end of the hall. Jerome stops dead in his tracks. There, front and center, is Jonah's big painting.

GYMNASIUM
We join a group of revelers as they enter the Halloween party.

PROFESSOR SANDIFORD (V.O.): Of all our holidays, none is so important to the art student as Halloween. It is on this occasion that the many divergent impulses found in all young artists—creativity, self-expression, and especially vanity and narcissism—join together to forge a seamless fusion in which, for this one night, the artist himself becomes a living work of art.

There are lots of goofy costumes, and way too many Frida Kahlos. We move our way through the crowd past Sandiford (dressed as Caesar) until we find Jerome, dressed as a clichéd "artist," with beret, and striped shirt. He approaches Vince, whose "costume" is an old fedora, and a familiar-looking blonde bombshell.

JEROME: Nice costume.

VINCE: What are you supposed to be? An old-time fag?

BLONDE: Aren't you going to introduce me to your charming friend?

VINCE: *(with a smirk)* Yeah Jerome, I'd like to you to meet my new friend, uh...

BLONDE: Serena.

VINCE: Serena.

She extends her hand, palm-down, for Jerome to kiss. Just as he is about to comply, he realizes that it's Matthew in drag.

JEROME: Oh, Jesus!

He drops the hand in disgust.

MATTHEW: *(with a haughty flip of the hair)* Well I never! Excuse me, gentlemen!

He sashays off. Audrey, dressed as a 1920s-style gun moll, enters. Jerome ditches Vince and goes to join her.

JEROME: Hi

AUDREY: Hi.

Candace approaches, dressed exactly as before.

CANDACE: *(to Audrey)* Remember when we came as slave and master? Those were the days.

AUDREY: No, they weren't.

JEROME: *(to Audrey)* Do you want something to drink? There's some weird orange punch over there.

AUDREY: Oh, how sweet. Thank you.

At the punch bowl, Jerome spots Bardo, dressed as a suburbanite, complete with Supercuts hairdo and golf pants. Professor Sandiford joins them.

PROFESSOR SANDIFORD: So, how are you fellows liking art school so far?

BARDO: *(deadpan)* Really great.

PROFESSOR SANDIFORD: *(to Jerome)* Sometimes you don't seem like you're too happy with the way the class is going, Jerome.

JEROME: No...it's okay...it's just—

PROFESSOR SANDIFORD: Look, I know how it is. Anyway, I just want you to know that I'm around if you ever want to talk. You can come by the studio and I'll put on a pot of tea and we can just shoot the shit if you want...you too, Bardo.

BARDO: *(again a wiseass)* Thank you, sir.

Sandiford moves on. Bardo nods toward Audrey.

BARDO (CONT'D): You better get back there, Platz; you're about to be cock-blocked by Joe College.

Jerome looks back to see that Audrey is talking to Jonah, who is dressed as an old-fashioned black-shirt-white-pinstripes-style gangster.

JEROME: What the fuck...

He hustles back with the drinks. As he approaches we hear:

AUDREY: *(To Jonah)* ...How did you ever do that painting? It's like you've never seen another painting in your life.

Jerome hands Audrey her drink.

AUDREY (CONT'D): Oh, thanks...

She stands next to Jonah, posing for Jerome.

AUDREY (CONT'D): Isn't it weird? Look how perfectly we match.

She turns away and resumes talking to Jonah. Candace moves next to Jerome.

CANDACE: Better luck next time, stud.

She pats him condescendingly on the back as Audrey and Jonah walk off.

CLASSROOM
Another class critique. Next to Jonah's latest (another big painting in the style of his earlier "Sports Car," this time of a viking ship) Jerome puts up a large canvas of his own, a painting of an old refrigerator. This one is more consciously childlike than his previous work; it looks like one of Jonah's, though with far more polish and finesse.

PROFESSOR SANDIFORD: *(amused)* It looks like a duel! Comments?

FLOWER: Jonah's seems totally original and authentic and Jerome's seems just lame.

VEGAN: Yeah, it's pathetic. *(looks back at Jerome)* No offense.

KISS-ASS: Yeah, it's like Jonah is tapping into this total childhood innocence...like he's got a whole way of seeing that's completely outside the box...and Jerome is totally in the box, y'know?

PROFESSOR SANDIFORD: Okay, okay, let's give Jerome a break. I mean, what he's trying to do is essentially impossible. You can't hope to sing in your own unique voice using someone else's vocal cords.

We see only the back of Jerome's head as he faces the class. Every muscle fiber throbs with suppressed anger.

CAMPUS

Close-up on a woman's face as she walks past the campus gate. Suddenly, she looks into the camera and her blank expression turns to one of extreme horror. She is being strangled. We see the whole scene from the attacker's perspective, all very messy and chaotic. Once the victim's body falls limp, she is dragged by her hair and left to die next to an overflowing trash bin. We hold on this image.

DORM ROOM

Dissolve to a grainy black-and-white photograph on the cover of a tabloid newspaper, which Vince waves around for emphasis while telling his roommates about the crime.

VINCE: Again, he picks a totally random victim. This chick was like a cashier, or something.

MATTHEW: How do they know it's the same guy?

VINCE: Oh come on, it's obvious—there's a million clues. For one thing—

MATTHEW: *(doesn't want to get into it)* That's okay, I believe you.

VINCE: Look at her—she was only thirty-one years old.

He holds up the paper and directs them to her photo with a somber glance.

VINCE (CONT'D): I mean, it's like a goddamn miracle ...I'm here bustin' my nuts to come up with a female character and this guy drops one right in my lap!

CLASSROOM

We see Audrey, alone, dressing behind the curtain in Sandiford's classroom (the main figure-drawing room). Just outside the door, two **ART-DORKS** *are talking.*

ART-DORK #1: Who'd you have for a model today? We got the Yeti again.

ART-DORK #2: Audrey.

ART-DORK #1: I never thought I'd say this, but I'm getting kinda sick of Audrey...I mean, I've seen her naked like 500 times.

ART-DORK #2: I know, she's been around forever.

ART-DORK #1: I'd still fuck her though.

In the corner of the room is an ever-growing pile of discarded art. We recognize several failed pieces from Sandiford's class, including Jerome's failed Jonah imitation. Audrey, disgusted, stomps past the dorks.

ART-DORK #2: Good job today, Audrey!

She can't even muster a dirty look. As she heads for the stairs, she notices a new painting in the hall gallery. It's Jonah's viking ship. She studies it with inscrutable dispassion.

DORM HALLWAY
Jerome is in the hallway, dialing a grimy communal pay phone. Towel-clad art-girls wander behind him. After several rings, Audrey answers.

JEROME: Hi, it's Jerome Platz.

We see Audrey in close-up talking on a cell phone.

AUDREY: Well, hello Jerome Platz.

JEROME: *(summoning every ounce of nerve)* I was just calling to...I...uh...I have to go home for Thanksgiving, and I was just wondering if you had any...if you possibly wanted to come with me. I know it's not for over a week, but I thought I'd ask you...

AUDREY: *(pause)* God, that's really sweet...

JEROME: I mean, you don't have to or anything, but I just thought I'd...

AUDREY: Yeah, unfortunately, I was just about to go up north to visit my Grandmother, but...God, that's really nice of you...

Jerome says goodbye and hangs up. Oh well. A wild-eyed **AMPHETAMINE-ADDICT** *runs out of his dorm room and grabs Jerome by the sleeve. He's someone we've seen fidgeting around in the background, but he's not in Sandiford's class.*

AMPHETAMINE ADDICT: Hey Jerome, I need your input on something.

Jerome follows him into his room. It looks like the aftermath of a tornado; everything has been smashed, overturned, strewn about.

JEROME: Do your roommates know about this?

AMPHETAMINE ADDICT: Not yet... *(pause)* So what do you think? Do you think I should hand this in?

BROADWAY BOB'S COFFEE HOUSE

We rejoin Audrey in a continuation of the previous scene. Her cell phone sits closed on the counter as she eats a piece of cake. Candace stands next to her waiting for take-out.

CANDACE: Don't you think that's a little creepy— to invite you home for Thanksgiving?

AUDREY: I guess it's a little weird, maybe...

CANDACE: You must emit some kind of hormone that attracts desperate, clingy losers.

AUDREY: I don't know...there's something about him...He always makes me feel like I'm on a date in Junior High, or something.

CANDACE: As I recall, you spent Junior High hanging out with a bunch of coked-out 35-year-old art dealers. I don't remember too many "dates."

AUDREY: Yeah, exactly.

CANDACE: Listen to me, Audrey: That guy is a total waste of time. Really, it just couldn't be more obvious. What's wrong with you that you can't see that?

AUDREY: You're right, I'm sure....

CANDACE: I thought you were all mad for that what's–his–name...Jonah.

AUDREY: I am, I think...

CANDACE: You don't need another boyfriend, you need about fifteen years of therapy!

AUDREY: This is going to be different—I'm really going to make it work this time.

CANDACE: Well, when this one doesn't work out, you can always come crawling back to me.

Candace surprises her with an unwanted kiss and quickly exits. Clearly, Audrey doesn't relish this prospect.

TRAIN CAR

Jerome sits quietly with his portfolio. The manic energy of the prior scene is replaced by an introspective stillness. Out of the crowd he spots a familiar face: It's Eugene, looking very Ivy League-ish. Next to him sits an attractive sorority girl.

EUGENE: Jesus, Jerome, is that you?

JEROME: Eugene?

EUGENE: What's up, man? *(off Jerome's look)* Oh... Jerome, this is Sarah. We're going to Mom's for Thanksgiving.

JEROME: *(stunned by Eugene's rapid climb from dork-hood)* Oh yeah, me too...I mean, I'm going to my house...you know...

EUGENE: You look really...interesting.

JEROME: Yeah, you too. What's—uh—what's up with you?

EUGENE: Nothing much...How about you? Still doing art and stuff?

JEROME: Yeah, you know...

They stare at each other, a million miles apart.

THE PLATZ FAMILY DINING ROOM

Jerome's family is seated around the Thanksgiving table. His parents are 50-ish New-Yorker-subscriber democrat suburbanites: decent folks who don't quite understand their son. Also present: His 16-year-old sister **CYNTHIA**, *a doddering* **AUNT**, *and* **CLIFFY**, *a chubby, 30-ish sports-fan cousin. A football game is on TV in the background and Cliffy fades in and out of the conversation depending on the score.*

CYNTHIA: So I've been thinking maybe I'll go on tour with Dominick's band this summer. They're going to play some shows in the Midwest and they need somebody to sell tee-shirts and stuff.

DAD PLATZ: Who is Dominick?

CYNTHIA: He's just this guy who's friends with Stacy's big brother.

MOM PLATZ: Forget about it.

CYNTHIA: God, you are so unfair! Jerome gets to go to art school and I can't even go on a summer trip!

There is a break in the game. Cliffy's attention shifts to Jerome, with whom he has a mild fascination.

CLIFFY: Hey Jerome, so you gonna get a job doin' paintings somewhere once you're done with school?

JEROME: No, that's not really how it works.

CYNTHIA: Who in their right mind would buy one of your stupid paintings?

MOM PLATZ: Cynthia.

CYNTHIA: God, why do you love Jerome so much more than me?

CLIFFY: You know what you gotta do, Jerome? You gotta figure out who's the top guy in your business and you gotta somehow hook up with him. 'Cause you know, Jerome, it's not what you do so much as who you know. That's how it is in my business, anyway... and hey, it's all business, right?

JEROME: *(enduring Cliffy's meaningless chatter)* Yep. *(then somewhat nervously, as though about to make an important announcement)* Yeah, in fact, I've—

CLIFFY: *(his attention diverted back to the game)* FUMBLE! What?!? What are you fucking crazy? That was out of bounds! Oh my God, you have got to be kidding me... *(then, calmly, back to Jerome)* No, I'm serious Jerome, if you can make the right connections, you got half the battle won right there. Anyway, that's my advice.

JEROME: Yeah well, I guess I've already made a few connections. My girlfriend's dad is kind of a famous artist...

Cynthia's fork stops an inch away from her open mouth.

CYNTHIA: Your what?

MOM PLATZ: *(to Dad)* Hugh, could you help me get the pies out of the oven?

They head for the kitchen. The second the door swings closed we hear muffled cheers.

CYNTHIA: We thought for sure you were a homo.

DODDERING AUNT: *(slowly, somewhat slurred)* My friend's granddaughter paints little pictures on the shoes...oh, what do they call them? She paints pictures of little animals and what-not on the shoes and I believe the other children pay her...Sneakers? Is that what they call them? Anyhow, that's just an idea of something you could do, Jeremy.

PROF'S APARTMENT
Jerome stands outside a nondescript building. Sandiford answers the door while talking on a cordless phone. He waves Jerome into a drab living room.

PROFESSOR SANDIFORD: *(on phone)* That's really bad news, Lorenzo, because I feel like I've just turned a corner with these new pieces...no, of course I understand completely, but isn't there...

His voice trails off as he wanders into another room. Jerome sits at a small table and looks around. A few moments later, **MRS. SANDIFORD,** *a worn-down, asexual faculty wife, enters carrying an artsy-fartsy tea service.*

MRS. SANDIFORD: I'm Helen Sandiford. Sandy will be right with you.

She serves him with the barely-polite distaste of one who has played host for way too many ungrateful students over the years.

JEROME: Oh wow, thank you, Mrs. Sandiford. I really appreciate—

She leaves, ignoring him. Jerome looks around. There are several unimpressive paintings on one wall.

PROFESSOR SANDIFORD (O.S.): Okay, fine Lorenzo... yes, you too. *(we hear him slam the cordless phone into the cradle, then, under his breath)* Go fuck yourself, Lorenzo!

Jerome, embarrassed, gets up to look at the paintings. Sandiford enters, regaining his composure.

PROFESSOR SANDIFORD (CONT'D): Those are mine, yes.

JEROME: They're really good...really great...

PROFESSOR SANDIFORD: Yes, I rather like them... *(then, bitterly)* Unfortunately, our opinion is not in the majority. I guess they're a little too difficult for some people.

JEROME: *(trying to fill the dead air)* So how long have you been doing the triangles?

PROFESSOR SANDIFORD: A long time...I was one of the first. *(then, shifting)* So, Jerome, what are you not getting from my class?

JEROME: Oh, it's not that at all…it's just, I feel like… I don't know, I'm not exactly sure what I should be doing…I feel like I need to establish my own style, or to—

PROFESSOR SANDIFORD: Oh that is such bullshit, Jerome. You kids are far too young to get all hung up on something like finding a "style."

JEROME: Well what about Jonah? He seems to have sort of a style.

PROFESSOR SANDIFORD: Jonah's work has a certain "nowness," but that doesn't make him a better artist— far from it—it's just that you and I, we're a different sort of animal…My god, do you know how long it's taken me to learn to paint like this?

JEROME: *(looking back at the triangles)* No…

PROFESSOR SANDIFORD: Twenty-five years!

JEROME: But I'm not like— *(catching himself)* I–I'm still confused…

PROFESSOR SANDIFORD (CONT'D): I can't tell you what to do, Jerome, but I can promise you this: Jonah does not stay awake at night thinking about what Jerome is doing. At your age, it's essential that you learn to experiment with all different kinds of art and philosophies and lifestyles.

JEROME: So you're saying I should try out a bunch of styles instead of just—

PROFESSOR SANDIFORD: Yes, yes, yes, Jerome! So many young artists get trapped in their own rigid way of thinking.

Jerome can't help but glance back at Sandiford's triangles. Sandiford sits next to him, a little too close.

JEROME: You think that's what I should try to do? Experiment?

PROFESSOR SANDIFORD: Absolutely.

Sandy places his hand on top of Jerome's.

PROFESSOR SANDIFORD (CONT'D): I hope I've been of some help to you, Jerome. I am here to facilitate your experimentation in any way I can, be it in or out of the classroom.

Jerome's look is one of newly-inspired determination, absolutely oblivious to the Professor's insinuations.

JEROME: Thank you, Professor.

MONTAGE
We see various students at work on their projects while bad rock music plays:
A pot-bellied fellow with a long, flowing mane wears a gold thong while posing in a full-length mirror for a very inept life-size self-portrait.
Mom, in her Martha Stewart-ish kitchen, puts the final touches on the worst painting ever.
An intense, bearded weirdo holds a camera at arms' length to take a photo of his own testicles.
Professor Zipkin stands in the amphetamine addict's trashed dorm room and nods approvingly at the carnage.

A paint-covered naked man throws himself at a gigantic canvas tacked to a wall, then writhes on the ground in extreme pain.

Amidst these, we see Jerome in various stages of work: Doing research, working in his studio, etc.

At the end of this sequence, a **CRANKY GUARD** *kicks Jerome and a few others out of the studio building.*

CRANKY GUARD: Go on, get out! Go home! Get out of my building!

Jerome struggles to keep the artwork from spilling out of his portfolio as the guard slams the door behind him.

COURTYARD

In the courtyard outside the gym, the students of the freshman class of the Fine Arts department mill around. A sign reads "POST-THANKSGIVING ASSESSMENT." A few idiots play hackey-sack. Jerome sits in silence next to Army-Jacket. Kiss-Ass comes bounding out of the gym.

KISS-ASS: He says they're all done. We can go in now.

GYMNASIUM

Jerome heads toward his display. His grade is tacked to the board, hidden by the overhang of a drooping canvas. He slowly lifts the canvas: IT'S AN A! Below that is tacked an envelope marked "comments." He grabs the envelope and, swelled with pride, marches through the hall. He spots Flower's display and pauses to check out her grade. Implausibly, she too has an A. He looks around—more As. Everyone seems to have an A. A guy whose entire display is a wadded-up paper towel has an A. He spots Jonah's display. He too has an A, but his is larger, and, unlike any of the others, lettered in red ink.

CAFETERIA

Jerome sits reading over his comment sheet. The horrible words echo in his head: "All over the map!" "Too experimental!" "Nothing to say" "Needs to be more provocative —shake things up!" A voice breaks through the reverberating din of words.

AUDREY: Hey...heads up, Platz.

He looks up to see Audrey smiling at him. She sits down, and begins to devour a large jelly donut.

AUDREY (CONT'D): So are you going to Marvin Bushmiller's birthday party?

JEROME: No...I didn't even know about it...

AUDREY: Oh, it might be an invite-only thing. It's probably all done through his gallery, so maybe they... *(trying to cover her gaffe)* I'm sure it'll be a total drag anyway.

JEROME: When is it?

AUDREY: Oh, I don't even know. I think it— *(she spots Jonah)* Hey! Over here!

JONAH: I can't believe it. I got an A.

JEROME: Everybody got an A. It's a total scam to trick everybody into feeling good about themselves.

JONAH: I never got better than a C my whole life.

JEROME: *(disdainfully)* That's hard to believe.

JONAH: Yeah, I guess I didn't go to class too much... too busy getting into trouble, y'know?

AUDREY: *(intrigued)* Really?

JEROME: *(trying to look equally tough)* Yeah, me too.

JONAH: Huh, no kidding. You grow up in the city?

JEROME: Not right in the city, but I came here all the time...all the fuckin' time...practically lived here...

JONAH: Yeah, then you know how it is...Yeah, I used to get into some pretty hard-core shit, I guess...

AUDREY: We've all made our share of mistakes, I'm sure...

JONAH: Yeah, no shit...no fucking shit... *(turns to Jerome)* So how about it, dude? You got any deep, dark secrets we should know about?

EDITING ROOM

The Beat Girl (Jerome's hysterical date) sits cross-legged on a stool, holding a script.

BEAT GIRL: *(Reading from the script; not a bad actress)* Murder?! Don't worry so much, man—nobody's going to murder me.

VINCE (O.S.): *(flat and slow)* I don't want nothing to happen to my best 'ho. The streets ain't safe no more. Not since—

BEAT GIRL: Fuck you! You're just trying to keep me down. And I'm not your whore any more! *(tries it again, with sarcastic emphasis)* I mean, "I'm not your whore no more." *(she lowers her script)* This is total shit, you know that?

We now see Vince and the rest of the room.

VINCE: *(stung)* No, I don't know that.

BEAT GIRL: Oh come on—all this gangsta mutha-fucka bullshit. What, are you going to play an ironically-happy pop song when I get strangled?

Vince looks at his shoes.

BEAT GIRL (CONT'D): Why do you want to regurgitate this Hollywood crap for the zillionth time? Don't you have anything original to say?

VINCE: I think I do.

BEAT GIRL: Then you need to say it! *(points at script)* This is completely worthless.

Her words hit Vince right in the gut.

TORSIELLO GALLERY
*They are putting up a new show; boxes and crates are everywhere. A fashionable young man is stencilling the words "MARVIN BUSHMILLER: A NEW DIRECTION" on a hardwood wall panel. Jerome looks around, gape-jawed at the impressive fixtures and luxurious furnishings. Every square inch conveys that this is truly the highest stratum of the art world. A middle-aged **ART DEALER** emerges from the back and glowers at the stencilled wall.*

ART DEALER: That's not working. Do it better. *(he notices Jerome)* We're closed.

He climbs a step-ladder to adjust some lights.

JEROME: Uh...Excuse me, I... *(he pauses for a second, changing his angle mid-sentence.)* I heard that Mr. Bushmiller is having a party this week and I was wondering if there was any possible way I could go.

ART DEALER: Sorry. Invite only.

JEROME: Look, I was going to tell you some elaborate lie, but I decided to be honest with you. I'm totally desperate. Isn't there anything you can do? I promise I'm not crazy. I won't even talk to Mr. Bushmiller at all. Please? I'll do anything...

ART DEALER: Look, as you can see we're very busy here, so—

Jerome drops to his knees.

JEROME: Please? Please? Please?

MARVIN BUSHMILLER'S APARTMENT

We see Jerome, wearing an embarrassing red uniform, tending bar. An impatient middle-aged **ART MATRON** *takes a sip from her drink and hands it back.*

ART MATRON: Did you put any Grenadine in this?

Jerome adds Grenadine. The woman wanders off, and for the first time Jerome has a chance to examine the setting: A beautiful, modern penthouse apartment filled with fashion mavens and art-world heavy-hitters. It's as though he's stepped directly into his most exaggerated fantasy. Despite the uniform, he is thrilled to be there. He covets this life so intensely he can barely stand it.

BIG GUY: Stoli and tonic.

Jerome makes it, and looks up to face the next person in line: It's Audrey. They recognize each other at precisely the same instant. Jerome has a line prepared for the occasion.

JEROME: I heard Marvin needed some help, so I figured why not?

Audrey seems embarrassed to see him and we immediately see why: Jonah is her date for the evening. Poor Jerome is crushed.

AUDREY: I...uh...I guess I'll have a Tom Collins.

Jerome glances at his open bar guide, and makes it without another word.

JONAH: Just a Bud is fine.

JEROME: *(without looking up)* We have Spaten and Hoegaarden.

JONAH: The first one.

There is an intense non-verbal exchange between the three of them. Audrey sips her drink and turns away, unable to sustain eye-contact with the defeated Jerome.

AUDREY: *(with sympathy and regret)* You look so busy. We'd better leave you alone for awhile.

They edge away.

NEXT IN LINE: Give me a Nuclear Holocaust.

JEROME: What's in that?

NEXT IN LINE: *(impatient)* I have no idea.

Jerome consults his book. He glances up to see Audrey, far across the room, introducing Jonah to Bushmiller, who warmly shakes his hand. Other party-goers are drawn to the radiant couple and they soon have a small crowd encircling them. Jerome scans past the bottles in the bar cabinet. His eyes land on a Sambuca label.

JIMMY'S VESTIBULE
He stands at Jimmy's door, pressing the buzzer.

JEROME: *(barking drunkenly)* It's Jerome...I'm Bardo's friend...I want to get shit-faced with you! Are you there? I brought a bottle of—

BZZZZT.

JIMMY'S APARTMENT

They sit, each with his own bottle. Jimmy uses a filthy cup, as is his way. He looks at the bottle.

JIMMY: I drink Slivovitz, not Sambuca.

He drinks it anyway.

JEROME: You were right about art. It's all about the cock-sucking.

JIMMY: It's not what you do, but who you blow.

JEROME: *(preoccupied, getting even madder)* And even that's not enough! They're lining up ten deep to suck cock! You don't even have a chance unless you're the most ruthless, cold-blooded—

Jerome lurches forward and vomits on the rug.

JEROME (CONT'D): Oh Jesus, I'm really sorry.

Jimmy hardly seems to notice. He tosses a newspaper on top of the offending splatter and sits back down. It's the same edition that Vince was reading earlier (with the story of the latest Strathmore murder). Jerome's befogged memory strains to make the connection. Jimmy notes his interest.

JIMMY: Have you heard about the great man's latest masterpiece?

JEROME: Huh?

JIMMY: It's some of his finest work, I believe. Damn good stuff!

JEROME: Who? The murderer?

JIMMY: Murderer? Tsk! That's so disrespectful.

JEROME: I've got a few victims for him if he's interested.

JIMMY: *(finishes off the cup with three slow gulps)* Do you want to see my paintings?

JIMMY'S STUDIO

They enter the studio, a windowless room wallpapered with twenty years of clippings, drawings, paintings, etc. Jimmy leads him to five small paintings tacked to the back wall. The paintings are crude portraits of the murder victims.

JIMMY: This is my humble tribute to the great man. He doesn't simply reproduce reality like an ordinary idiot artist, he courageously reshapes it to suit his own needs!

Jerome nods, too drunk to fully grasp the extent of Jimmy's nuttiness.

JIMMY (CONT'D): And why did our great artist select these particular victims? Who can say? A real artist knows when he has found his ideal subject! *(pointing at each canvas in turn)* Perhaps this one was a DISHONEST CASHIER...this one might have reminded him of a DOMINEERING AUNT...and this one—maybe he was just TOO STUPID TO BE ALLOWED TO LIVE!

JEROME: All of humanity is too stupid to live!

Jimmy looks at him, somewhat impressed.

JEROME (CONT'D): *(too loud)* Fuck them all!

Jimmy puts his hand on Jerome's shoulder.

JIMMY: My boy!

JIMMY'S APARTMENT
They are back in the living room. Jerome is really out of it.

JIMMY: ...I say you can't do anything really good until you truly don't care at all if you live or die. Kill me right now, I couldn't care less. It's only when every human misery is just a big joke that you can finally get some enjoyment out of this life.

JEROME: I wish someone would kill me right now.

JIMMY: Do you want me to kill you?

JEROME: Go for it.

JIMMY: *(an evil pause)* Oh my gosh, the bottle's empty.

JEROME: I guess I better go before I throw up on your rug again.

Jerome stumbles toward the door, Jimmy grabs him by the shoulders and holds him for a tense moment.

JIMMY: Wait! I want to give you something.

He heads back into the studio and returns with a rolled-up canvas. He hands it to Jerome with a pat on the back.

JEROME: What's this?

JIMMY: A gift from me to you.

JEROME: Oh no, I couldn't.

JIMMY: You could, you could.

BAD NEIGHBORHOOD

Jerome stumbles past a graffiti-covered dumpster. He lifts the lid to throw away Jimmy's painting, but somehow can't quite let it go. He unrolls a few inches and looks at it with drunken intrigue.

SCHOOL STUDIO

Jerome staggers into the studio building. The cranky guard stops him.

CRANKY GUARD: Let's see your I.D.

JEROME: Huh?

CRANKY GUARD: I.D.!

Jerome fumbles for it.

CRANKY GUARD (CONT'D): Are you drunk?

JEROME: No way.

He glances at his card and lets him go. Jerome rounds a corner and we immediately hear a loud splatter as he pukes on the plastic floor. He enters his cubicle and unrolls Jimmy's canvas. It's one of Jimmy's murder victim portraits, The Dishonest Cashier. He pins it to the wall next to the original figure-drawing of Audrey. Jimmy's is a hideous, anger-distorted, dorian-gray version of its counterpart. He notices that the victim's obituary is pasted to the canvas, along with what looks like her business card.

He looks at the drawing of Audrey and starts to cry. He kisses her on the lips.

AUDREY'S APARTMENT
Jerome is sitting on the pavement outside Audrey's apartment. Audrey emerges from the front door and checks her mailbox. Jerome approaches.

JEROME: Hi.

AUDREY: *(startled)* God, you scared me.

JEROME: *(still drunk)* I just wanted to see you.

AUDREY: Jesus Christ, Jerome, you're a mess...A guy like you can't just start drinking like you're Jackson Pollock in one night...

JEROME: A guy like me...

AUDREY: Come on...you need to sober up.

BROADWAY BOB'S COFFEE HOUSE

They sit in a booth. Jerome looks dishevelled and wild-eyed.

AUDREY: What are you doing, Jerome?

JEROME: I just don't get what you could possibly see in that stupid jock asshole.

AUDREY: I don't "see" anything. He's just a friend… *(pause)* like you are.

JEROME: Like I am!

She touches his trembling hand.

AUDREY: Yes.

JEROME: You and I have something—there's something between us…you can't just ignore it, there's something there, there's a—

AUDREY: Have you ever had a real girlfriend, Jerome?

JEROME: No, because I never felt this way about anybody ever before!

AUDREY: I just don't think you really—

JEROME: You cannot think that jerk is a great artist! I know you don't believe that...

AUDREY: You really shouldn't worry about what I think. I'm not worth it.

JEROME: Yes, you are.

AUDREY: I'm just as shallow as everybody else. I mostly base my opinion of an artist on what other people say, or how much their work sells for, or all that superficial nonsense.

JEROME: No, you don't..

AUDREY: *(trying to let him down easy)* Sometimes I'm not even sure if I give a shit about art at all. I mean, who cares? Who needs it? Nobody.

JEROME: Will you be my girlfriend?

AUDREY: Jerome...

Jerome's eyes fill immediately with tears, though his expression remains oddly numb.

AUDREY (CONT'D): Look at you, you really are a mess.

JEROME: If you see that jock asshole, tell him I will bury him! I will bury him alive and shit on his grave!!

MUSEUM
Audrey and Jonah are sitting in an otherwise unoccupied museum gallery. Judging by the art, we are apparently in the Modern Wing.

AUDREY: So what's your favorite painting of all time?

JONAH: *(thinks for a minute)* Maybe the Mona Lisa.

AUDREY: *(laughs)* You're so funny! The sad thing is that's probably what most people would say.

JONAH: I know...It's fucking pathetic.

She moves a little closer to him.

AUDREY: How come a guy like you doesn't have a million girlfriends?

JONAH: I don't like to be tied down, I guess.

AUDREY: Never?

JONAH: *(looks at her)* No, not never.

Audrey slides even closer.

AUDREY: You're very mysterious, you know.

Suddenly, Jonah is overcome. They kiss.

JONAH: I guess you could say I have an interest in, like, the dark side of humanity.

AUDREY: Me too.

JONAH: Yeah, you strike me as a girl who knows where all the bodies are buried.

AUDREY: *(a pause)* Oh, God, don't say that.

JONAH: What?

AUDREY: Nothing...It's just something somebody said that really creeped me out...

JONAH: What?

AUDREY: It was something like "I will bury you and shit on your grave."

JONAH: *(concerned)* Somebody said that to you?

AUDREY: It was just something Jerome said...I mean, he didn't really say it to me, it was just—he was really freaked-out, you know. He—

JONAH: When was this?

AUDREY: Don't worry...It's nothing...I'm sure I'm totally overreacting...

JONAH: I'm just concerned for the guy, that's all. He hasn't been coming to class, y'know, and I just wonder what—

AUDREY: *(she touches his arm)* God, that's really amazing. Most artists are so self-centered.

DIVE BAR
Jerome sits alone at the bar, drinking film-noirishly. In the background we see a table of art-girls, and a few locals playing pool/pinball. Bardo enters.

BARDO: Well look who's here. Where have you been all week?

JEROME: I've just been having a really hard time.

BARDO: Look, you should just do what I always do— drop out and start over again next semester. This is my third time...soon to be my fourth...

Jerome glances at him.

BARDO (CONT'D): Yeah, I've pretty much had it with Sandy's class. I'm thinking of switching over to video. *(a beat)* I mean, we may as well stay in school as long as we can. We can't be artists forever.

JEROME: You don't understand...I'll never have another chance like this. I can't just start over...I'll never find another Audrey...

BARDO: Oh, please...don't start with that again...

He notices the locals trying to make time with the art-girls.

JEROME: Every artist needs a subject; she's my perfect subject. I can't let her slip through my fingers...

BARDO: C'mon, let's go rescue these art-chicks. That's easy pickin's.

JEROME: *(doesn't even hear him)* I know I can get her back if I can just come up with something for that final survey. I need to get their attention, that's all. They'll forget all about Jonah.

BARDO: *(eyeing girls)* Yeah, yeah...C'mon, we're gonna miss our chance.

JEROME: I've got to think of something. I know I'm better than that jerk...I know it...

The art-girls escape.

BARDO: There they go.

JEROME: What should I do? There has to be something...

He makes direct eye-contact with Bardo, desperate for any kind of human understanding.

BARDO: You know, I think I finally figured out who you are.

JEROME: Who?

BARDO: You're the class douche-bag.

He leaves. Jerome drains the last drop from his glass. He notices, in the far corner booth, a solitary figure with her face buried in her hands. It's Sophie, his art history professor. He wanders over and sits undetected at her table. There are several empty glasses in front of her, along with a thick notebook open to a page of scribbled ball-point text.

JEROME: *(concerned)* What's wrong?

SOPHIE: *(looks up, a little startled)* Do I know you?

JEROME: I'm in your Tuesday/Thursday class.

SOPHIE: Oh God...

JEROME: I know how you feel.

SOPHIE: You couldn't possibly know how I feel.

JEROME: You're right. I'm sorry...All I meant was... What's wrong? Did your husband leave you?

SOPHIE: What?

JEROME: I totally understand. I've been going through the same kind of—

SOPHIE: My husband left me fifteen years ago. Thank God. Now if you'll please go away, I'd like to get back to my work.

JEROME: *(looks at scribbled notebook)* Are you writing a book?

She glares at him.

JEROME (CONT'D): Is it about art?

SOPHIE: No, it's about you.

JEROME: Me?

SOPHIE: Your kind. Your ilk. It's about your failure to create anything of lasting value and the ugliness and impurity of your motives. It's about my despair over your inability to move me, or thrill me, or to engage even the simplest human emotion. It's really quite a nasty book, I'm afraid.

JEROME: *(sincere)* I'd love to read it.

SOPHIE: Well, aren't you a good sport.

She looks him over with art-critic scrutiny.

SOPHIE (CONT'D): What do you want?

JEROME: Do you miss him?

SOPHIE: Who?

JEROME: Your husband.

SOPHIE: *(thinks about it for a moment, then, dropping her guard)* Yes, sometimes. *(a tiny pause)* But at least I have my cats.

SCHOOL STUDIO
Jerome enters the studio. The cranky guard is asleep, snoring loudly. Jerome heads down the dark hallway, but stops suddenly when he sees a light coming from his own cubicle. He edges closer and peers through a crack—it's Jonah, rummaging through his stuff! Jonah takes out a

small digital camera and takes several pictures. Jerome accidentally kicks a coffee can filled with brushes, startling Jonah, who hastily pockets the camera and sneaks off.

HALLWAY

As Jerome heads toward class, Army-Jacket rolls up on his skateboard. He does annoying tricks while he talks.

ARMY-JACKET: So, it looks like you've finally got Jonah on the run.

JEROME: What do you mean?

ARMY-JACKET: He was asking about some painting of yours. You got a big surprise for us at the final survey?

JEROME: *(thinks)* I don't know.

CLASSROOM

Prof. Sandiford stands before the class amid a sparse accumulation of last-minute projects.

PROFESSOR SANDIFORD: The reason we have you put up your work in the Post-Thanksgiving Assessment is to give you a chance to make improvements and adjustments before the Final Survey, but we can't help you if you don't bring anything to class...this means you, Jerome! Don't give up on me!

JEROME: I'm working on something...

PROFESSOR SANDIFORD: No secrets in this class, young man!

A few of the students look at Jerome, intrigued by the notion of his "secret painting." A "buzz" is starting to develop. Jerome and Jonah exchange brief eye-contact. The professor approaches Jonah's latest.

PROFESSOR SANDIFORD (CONT'D): Nice stuff, Jonah... We're expecting big things from you at the final survey!

KISS-ASS: So you're saying that Jonah's the only one with a chance at the best grade?

PROFESSOR SANDIFORD: No, of course not.

SHILO: That's what it sounds like.

ARMY-JACKET: Professor Okamura says you'd have sex with your own mother's corpse to have a student with the best grade.

PROFESSOR SANDIFORD: Larry must be talking about himself. My mother is very much alive.

SCHOOL STUDIO
It's very late and Jerome has the building to himself. He is working on his own version of a "murder painting," which he has pinned up next to Jimmy's Cashier painting for reference. It's not going well. Suddenly, the door squeaks open. Jerome quickly tears down the two paintings and hides them under his supply table. The filthy-haired girl walks by his cubicle. He just stands there, smiling awkwardly.

FILTHY-HAIRED GIRL: What?

JEROME: Nothing. *(a pause)* How ya doin'?

FILTHY-HAIRED GIRL: Forgot my cigarettes.

She fetches them quickly and stomps out.

FILTHY-HAIRED GIRL (CONT'D): *(as she leaves)* You're weird.

He re-pins the paintings and gets back to work. Time passes: We see him get more and more discouraged in several dissolves. He just can't capture the angry, chaotic affect of Jimmy's original. Finally, he yanks what has become a hopeless, muddy eye-sore from the wall and crumples it in disgust.

JIMMY'S APARTMENT DOORWAY
An especially groggy-looking Jimmy unlatches the bolt-lock and faces him.

JIMMY: What do you want?

JEROME: *(seething and desperate)* I need a big favor.

Jimmy stumbles back inside. Jerome enters behind him.

JIMMY: I see you've come empty-handed.

JEROME: I know, I'm sorry, I—

JIMMY: You must think I'm the cheapest whore in town.

Jimmy sits on the couch, barely able to keep his eyes open. Jerome is too fidgety to sit still. He moves from chair to table, nervously chain-lighting a cigarette from the previous butt.

JEROME: I'll bring you a case of Slivovitz...or whatever you want...I want to buy the rest of your paintings.

JIMMY: They're not for sale.

JEROME: Please, just tell me what you want.

JIMMY: I don't want anything.

JEROME: I–I just—

JIMMY: I thought you were an artist.

JEROME: I–I am...I just—

JIMMY: Do you want to be an artist or an "aficionado"?

JEROME: An artist...

JIMMY: What do you think the artist cares about? Does he think all day about fine wines and black-tie affairs and what he's going to say at the next after-dinner speech?

There is a long pause as Jimmy closes his eyes. It seems for a moment that he might have fallen asleep.

JIMMY (CONT'D): No! He lives only for that narcotic moment of creative bliss! A moment that may come once a decade, or never at all! You think I'm wrong?

Jerome shakes his head "no."

JIMMY (CONT'D): FUCK YOU!! YOU KNOW NOTHING AT ALL!! ABOUT ANYTHING!!

JEROME: I don't care about fine wines. I just want— I don't know, I want...

There is a long pause as Jimmy stares at the floor. His demeanor changes and for a brief moment he actually seems vulnerable, full of sadness and regret.

JIMMY: I know what you want. I was once like you... *(he looks Jerome in the eye)* If it was me, I'd get my way by any means possible. I'd grab them by the balls and I'd never stop twisting. Once you're on top, they're helpless—you've got them squirming under the toe of your shoe!

JEROME: But...

Jimmy starts to cough.

JIMMY: Will you PLEASE put out that god-damned cigarette before you kill me with your awful smoke!!

He launches into a horrible red-faced coughing fit. Jerome makes an attempt to snuff out his cigarette in a tea-cup on the edge of the sofa, but he still has only one thing on his mind. He waits for a brief pause in the coughing.

JEROME: What about the paintings?

Jimmy curls up, exhausted, in a fetal ball on the couch.

JIMMY: I don't care. Do whatever you want.

He lies motionless with his back to Jerome, breathing softly. Jerome's cigarette is still smoldering in the tea-cup. He fishes it out and revives it with a long drag. He puts it back in the precariously-balanced cup and disappears into the hallway that leads to Jimmy's studio.

JIMMY'S STUDIO
Jerome rolls the paintings into a tube and looks around for a rubber band. He settles for a small piece of rope hanging from a hook. As he leaves, he notices what looks like Bardo's stocking cap pinned to the wall.

EDITING ROOM
Cut to VIDEO. As a loud, operatic score builds to its climax, we see a colorful series of slickly-edited cuts:
Sped-up stock footage of soldiers marching.
The Beat Girl doing an angry interpretive dance (also sped-up).

Jerome and Audrey's kiss, manipulated with cheap video effects.
An overly dramatic shot of the strangler on his knees, begging the heavens for mercy.
A slow-motion shot of the Beat Girl being doused with a bucket of blood.
A writhing mass of earthworms.
We then see the audience for this cinematic extravaganza: Vince, Jason, a smiling Beat Girl, and a sour-looking old man wearing large aviator glasses. This is Vince's **GRANDPA.** *The music crescendos and fades. Jason gets up to turn on the lights.*

GRANDPA: *(after a dyspeptic pause)* What the hell was that?

VINCE: Don't worry—it's totally a rough cut, and that's just a temp score without any—

GRANDPA: I thought you were going to make a nice little murder picture, but here you've got the worms and the dancing... *(turns to Jason)* Did you like it?

VINCE: It's symbolism, grandpa!

GRANDPA: And where are the guns? I thought this was supposed to be a shoot-em-up!

VINCE: The guy's a strangler, grandpa—what am I supposed to do?

GRANDPA: I want guns!

VINCE: That's the name of the movie—The Strathmore Strangler! You want The Strangler to shoot people?!

GRANDPA: I paid for a movie with guns!

DORM ROOM

Jerome looks at the five murder paintings laid out on his desk. It's the first time he's really had a chance to study them. One of them has a lock of hair taped to it; another has what looks like the victim's actual driver's license glued to the corner. Jerome picks at it, unsure as to how the likes of Jimmy could have fabricated such a convincing facsimile. Matthew enters and sits. He seems troubled.

MATTHEW: Can I talk to you about something?

JEROME: *(not listening)* Sure...

MATTHEW: I–I have a confession to make.

JEROME: Yeah?

MATTHEW: Oh, forget it.

JEROME: *(turns and tries to show some interest)* What?

MATTHEW: Nothing. Forget I said anything.

JEROME: What is it? Some boyfriend problem?

MATTHEW: What!? Why?

JEROME: I don't know...what is it then?

MATTHEW: Why did you say that?! Do you think I'm gay?!

JEROME: I don't know...

MATTHEW: Really?

JEROME: Yeah, maybe, I guess....

MATTHEW: Yeah, well, that's it. That's my confession: I think I'm gay.

JEROME: Okay.

MATTHEW: Okay

Jerome shakes his head and returns to the paintings.

FIGURE DRAWING CLASS
Professor Zipkin finishes measuring the clavicle of a partially-draped Audrey with giant wooden calipers as he addresses the class.

PROFESSOR ZIPKIN: ...of course, not everyone has such bone symmetry. Remember that ridiculous old crone they sent in here last week? My god, what a creature! *(he breaks into a weird laugh)* That's all for this week. Thank you, my dear.

Audrey covers up and escapes behind her curtain in the corner. It is the same classroom that Professor Sandiford uses. She emerges to lace up her shoes, propping her foot on a discarded sculpture in the now-enormous corner pile of abandoned art. She looks down to see a painting of her Little Audrey necklace sticking out from the bottom of the heap. She yanks it out, causing a small avalanche. It's Jerome's color portrait of Audrey, covered with footprints and charcoal dust. She brushes it with her sleeve and stares at it for a very long time.

JONAH'S APARTMENT STUDIO

Jonah is painting, his face contorted in a Mick Jagger-ish scowl. Top forty rock blares from a small clock-radio. The shot widens and we see that he's in a small room in a modern apartment. A youngish woman enters, carrying a handful of plastic baby toys. This is Jonah's wife, **MARIE.**

MARIE: I thought you said you were working?

JONAH: I am working. I gotta have this done for Monday.

MARIE: It doesn't have to be perfect, Jonah—it looks fine...

JONAH: It's got a long way to go.

MARIE: I don't know what's gotten into you, Jonah. When you were working narcotics you didn't spend all your off-hours smoking crack... *(a baby cries off screen)* Listen to your son, Jonah. He misses his Daddy.

JONAH: Will you get off my ass for once.

She glares at him, swallowing an angry outburst.

MARIE: Lonny and the guys are here to see you, or are you too busy for them, too?

JONAH: Alright, I'm coming...

JONAH'S APARTMENT LIVING ROOM

Jonah enters the living room, wiping his hands with a rag. **LONNY** *is Jonah's boss, a 45-ish detective. With him are* **KEVIN** *and* **MIKEY**, *his tough-guy underlings. Marie takes the baby from his bassinet and rocks him to stop the crying.*

KEVIN: Well look who's here. How's the Mona Lisa comin', Rembrandt?

MIKEY: Hey, Jonah, you're off duty—you don't have to dress like a fruitcake today.

JONAH: Yeah, great to see you guys, too.

MARIE: How much longer is this gonna go on, Lonny? I never see him anymore since he became an artist.

JONAH: I'm just trying to do my job, okay?

LONNY: That's a good question, Marie. So how 'bout it, superstar? We got the blow-ups of those pictures you took.

He takes out a sheath of digital prints of the Cashier painting.

LONNY (CONT'D): It's not much, but it looks like he uses the same pigments—

MIKEY: The what??

LONNY: Pigments, dumbass. The paint colors. He used the same combination of colors that we found on the glove at the first crime scene. *(points)* It's like vermill—uh ver—

JONAH: Vermillion.

LONNY: I don't know about this guy, though...he didn't live around campus when the first two killings took place...

JONAH: He used to come to the city all the time—he told me so himself...I just need a little more time to—

MIKEY: It would've been a big help if you could've taken a paint sample...

JONAH: You can't just mess around with a piece of art...I mean, I didn't want to—

Jonah stops himself—he can't believe he's saying this.

MIKEY: A piece of shit is more like it! Look at this fuckin' thing! *(aside)* 'Scuse me, Marie...Are you tellin' me we can't at least drag this asshole in for questioning? It's like he's makin' fun of us!

LONNY: Listen to me, tough-guy—I'm still getting shit to this day about that other weirdo we dragged in. We cannot afford another fuck-up. *(aside)* 'Scuse me, Marie...Y'gotta get me some better shit, Jonah.

MIKEY: The whole thing is fucked-up—the public is way too involved in this thing as it is.

KEVIN: What about the phone call?

MIKEY: Big deal—some guy calls and says "I will shit on you."

LONNY: "I will bury you alive and shit on your grave." It was him—he wanted his glove back.

This hits Jonah. He starts to say something, but stops himself. They get up to leave. Lonny looks back at Jonah, for whom he clearly has a fatherly affection.

LONNY (CONT'D): Hey, thanks, superstar...Don't work too hard.

Jonah nods stoically.

KEVIN: Don't go swish on us, okay?

They leave.

MARIE: I have to give Brandon his bath. Can you run to the store for me?

JONAH: *(as he walks back to his "studio")* Yeah, in a minute; I'm almost done.

JONAH'S APARTMENT STUDIO
He picks up a brush and looks at his painting. He turns up the volume on the clock-radio, and all of a sudden he's an artist again.

BROADWAY BOB'S COFFEE HOUSE

Jerome sits at the counter drinking coffee. Broadway Bob enters, yelling into his cell phone.

BROADWAY BOB: Listen to me, Gerry...Gerry! Will you listen?...Look, I know you're a genius, but I'm a genius too...Listen to me—this guy is going to make you a fortune...I'm a hundred percent on this one, Gerry... What?! How dare you talk to me like that you *(fades out as he enters his office).*

Jerome spots a lonely figure in the corner booth. It's Sophie, hard at work on her manuscript. She exasperatedly crosses out a long sentence and massages her brow, as though deep in thought. Jerome wanders over.

JEROME: *(points to the notebook)* How's it going?

She looks up, ready to admonish whoever might dare to disturb her, but she softens when she recognizes Jerome.

SOPHIE: I'm almost done with the first page.

JEROME: I'm dying to know what happens to me.

SOPHIE: I'll be sure to let you know.

JEROME: Can I ask you a question?

She nods toward the open seat. He sits.

JEROME (CONT'D): So there's this Freshman Survey tomorrow...

SOPHIE: And you want to know what you can do to land a big gallery contract like Marvin Bushmiller....

JEROME: Yeah...I mean, no...not exactly...

SOPHIE: Perhaps you want a major retrospective at the Metropolitan?

JEROME: No, it's just...there's somebody who I...I don't know, I want her to...

SOPHIE: It's for a girl?

JEROME: Yeah.

SOPHIE: You want to take the prize so you can win the heart of a girl?

We see that, for once, she's absolutely sincere.

JEROME: Exactly.

SOPHIE: Oh, that's so exciting.

JEROME: Will you...could you maybe come look at my paintings and tell me if they're good enough to win?

She takes his hand and smiles with genuine affection.

SOPHIE: No, but I'm rooting for you.

MONTAGE

In her studio cubicle,the basketball bull-dyke puts the finishing touches on a gigantic paper-maché ice cream cone. The intense-looking, bearded weirdo (from the pre-Thanksgiving montage) looks admiringly at an entire wall of large blow-up photos of his testicles.
Professor Sandiford's hand makes a big black X on the day before the final survey on his wall calendar.

DORM ROOM

Jerome lies in the darkness, fully dressed on top of his sheets; he's wound up like a spring.

CAMPUS

Audrey enters the campus gate and heads toward the gym. Our two detectives, Kevin and Mikey, watch her from an unmarked sedan as they eat their way through a bag of White Castle hamburgers.

MIKEY: You think Jonah's gettin' any gash on the side?

KEVIN: Nah, Marie's got him so pussy-whipped it's not even funny.

He slurps his orange soda and downs another burger.

MIKEY: Hey, there's our guy!

Jerome walks by, carrying a portfolio. He has a slightly deranged, sleepless look in his eye.

MIKEY (CONT'D): Look at him...boy, I'd like to break his scrawny neck right now. What are we waiting for?

KEVIN: He doesn't look like he could strangle a fuckin' cat.

MIKEY: Fucking scumbag...

KEVIN: Where the fuck is Jonah at? Lonny told him to be on the guy's ass all day...

MIKEY: "Like a fuckin' hemorrhoid, Jonah." I heard him myself.

GYMNASIUM

Inside, Jonah is putting up his paintings, fussily rearranging the display. In the far background we see Jerome walk past. He heads over to his assigned area and stands there for a moment, mumbling to himself. He takes a breath and begins to pin Jimmy's murder paintings to the display easel. A small crowd gathers, keeping a respectful distance. Once finished, he heads to the men's room, leaving the crowd free to swarm forward.

MEN'S ROOM

It's unbelievably filthy, covered floor-to-ceiling with graffiti. Jerome pees. A shadow appears, and we hear the sound of a second urine stream. It's Jonah. They both pee for what seems like an eternity before Jonah finally breaks the silence.

JONAH: Hey man, good luck out there today!

JEROME: Yeah, you too!

Jonah finishes and exits. Jerome continues to pee for what has now been a Guinness Book length of time. He stops and goes to the sink. He splashes water on his face and tries to fabricate an air of confidence.

GYMNASIUM

Jerome walks toward his display. Eno, Shilo, and Army-Jacket walk toward him, shaking their heads.

ENO: Jesus, that was disappointing.

ARMY-JACKET: Yeah, really Jerome...who are you trying to fool with all that bad-ass stuff?

SHILO: All that murder shit is totally September tenth, Jerome.

They walk away, leaving the shell-shocked Jerome alone in the middle of the auditorium. Prof. Sandiford approaches from the other side.

PROFESSOR SANDIFORD: Jerome, have you seen Jonah?

Jerome can't even respond.

PROFESSOR SANDIFORD (CONT'D): *(with fabricated sympathy)* Oh, and hey—better luck next time. *(he walks away)* Call me over the break and we'll figure out how to get you back on track.

Jerome spots Audrey across the room. He starts toward her, but retreats when he sees her join the crowd around Jonah's display. He glances back at his own display, which has but one remaining observer—Jonah. We join Jonah. He is furtively collecting paint samples with a small set of tweezers. As Jerome stomps toward him, Jonah deftly pockets the evidence.

JEROME: Okay, you win! It's all yours so live it up!

JONAH: Jerome, I—

JEROME: You're the one-out-of-a-hundred who goes on to fame and fortune, and I'm obviously just another deluded asshole.

JONAH: These paintings—

JEROME: Fuck those fucking paintings and fuck you! You may have everybody else fooled, but not me!

JONAH: Look, Jerome, I—

JEROME: You came up with a good gimmick, and you got them to buy your little tough-guy Joe Normal act, but your paintings are fucking bullshit and you know it!!

JONAH: Yeah, well, I still kicked your ass.

Jerome doesn't respond—Jonah is absolutely right. Prof. Sandiford rounds the corner.

PROFESSOR SANDIFORD: There you are, Jonah! Get over here!

JONAH: Jerome, wait here—I want to talk to you.

Sandiford drags him away.

PROFESSOR SANDIFORD: Your public awaits!

Jonah looks back anxiously at Jerome who just stands there, frozen in despair. Jonah is mobbed by well-wishers, most notably Hector, Broadway Bob's henchman.

HECTOR: *(hands him an official-looking card)* My employer, Mr. Broadway Bob D'Annunzio, requests that you join him at his establishment forthwith to discuss the possibility of an art exhibition.

A cheer rises from the crowd. Sandiford spots a dejected Okamura standing off to the side.

PROFESSOR SANDIFORD: Cheer up, Larry. There's always next year.

Audrey emerges to join Jonah in celebration. Suddenly his smile shifts to concern and he looks back over his shoulder. Jerome is gone.

BAD NEIGHBORHOOD
Jerome rounds a corner holding a brown paper bag from which he extracts a large bottle of Slivovitz. He twists open the cap and takes a big gulp as he stomps along.

GYMNASIUM
The crowd has thinned. Lonny, Jonah's boss, stands off to the side talking to Professor Zipkin who consults a xeroxed floor plan and points him toward Jerome's display. Lonny goes over to take a look. He stands transfixed. He picks at the I.D. card. He can't believe it—this is practically a confession.

LONNY: *(under his breath)* What the fuck, Jonah!

He grabs his walkie-talkie.

LONNY (CONT'D): Mikey! Get your ass over here! Where's Jonah?

CAMPUS

Jonah surveys the campus looking frantically for Jerome. Audrey tugs at his sleeve.

AUDREY: We should go, Jonah…Bob hates it when people are late.

JONAH: You don't understand—I really have to find Jerome…

AUDREY: Don't worry about Jerome. He'll be okay.

She grabs Jonah's hand and pulls him toward the campus gate. He takes one last look over his shoulder. In front of them in the distance, two men emerge from behind a building. The first man looks frightened and starts to run away. The second man takes out a gun and shoots him in the back. Jonah freezes for a moment, and then, unable to suppress his policeman's training, runs at top speed and tackles the gunman. The victim, apparently unhurt, rises and grabs Jonah from behind—we recognize him as Jason, Vince's sidekick. The gunman is the cranky security guard. Leslie and Hurst, armed with sound gear, come out of nowhere to join the fray. It's a moment of total chaos. Jonah takes out his badge and begins to yell in a

160

drill-instructor voice.

JONAH: POLICE! GET ON THE GROUND NOW! GET ON THE GROUND!

His three nemeses cower before him. We hear yelling from off-screen. Jonah looks to see Vince, holding his camera, screaming from a second-story window. There are several other crew members hiding in the bushes.

VINCE: WHAT ARE YOU DOING, ASSHOLE!?

CRANKY GUARD: *(whimpering)* My arm! I think my arm is broken!!

VINCE: THAT'S JUST GREAT! WHAT IN FUCK'S NAME AM I GONNA DO NOW?!

Jonah turns to face Audrey. All the life has been drained from her face. She takes a step back.

JONAH: Audrey, I...

AUDREY: Please tell me you're not a fake...

JONAH: I'm real...I'm totally real...

Kevin comes running toward them.

KEVIN: Let's go, hot-shot! The chief wants you right now!

He drags Jonah away from the scene. Jonah takes one last look at Audrey and realizes in that instant that he's back to his old life again; he's Jonah, the cop.

DORM HALLWAY
Mikey is pounding on the cheap, hollow door to Jerome's dorm room.

MIKEY: Police! Open the door! I have a warrant!

He rattles the knob and gives it a good push. The cheap-o lock breaks and the door bursts open. He barges in, gun drawn.

MIKEY (CONT'D): Police! Don't try anythi—

He stops dead.

MIKEY (CONT'D): Oh Jesus.

Matthew and the Leather Cross-straps guy are cowering naked on the bed. Mikey is just as scared as they are.

MATTHEW: This isn't what you think!

The cross-straps guy gives him a look. It isn't? Mikey notices a short piece of rope on the floor, which we recognize as the rope Jerome used to tie up Jimmy's paintings. He reaches for it.

MATTHEW (CONT'D): Did my parents send you?

BAD NEIGHBORHOOD

Jerome passes the now-familiar graffiti-covered dumpster adjacent to Jimmy's building. He heads for the door, but it's all boarded-up, covered with yellow hazard tape and fire damage stickers. He looks around to make sure he's on the right block. The building is covered with black soot, and all the windows are either blown out or boarded up. A ten-year-old **KID** *wanders over.*

KID: The building burned up and all the people died.

JEROME: Everybody?

KID: Yep.

Jerome is speechless. He stares at Jimmy's charred window.

KID (CONT'D): Some asshole didn't put out his cigarette.

Jerome looks at the kid. He hands him his bottle of Slivovitz. He then takes out his wallet and gives the kid all his cash, about thirty bucks, and his ATM card.

JEROME: This is my bank card. I think I have about four hundred bucks in there. My PIN number is 10–25–1881. It's Picasso's birthday. You should go to the museum and see some of his paintings sometime; he's really good.

The kid is awe-struck. Jerome tosses his wallet in the trash and walks back toward campus.

BROADWAY BOB'S COFFEE HOUSE
Broadway Bob waits impatiently.

BROADWAY BOB: So what—this fucking nobody is going to stand me up?

HECTOR: I gave him the message, Mr. D'Annunzio.

BROADWAY BOB: Yeah, well, he just officially missed his big chance. Fuck him, and fuck Sandy Sandiford.

GYMNASIUM

A forensic team collects evidence from Jerome's display, as a growing crowd looks on. We see Prof. Zipkin talking to a crest-fallen Sandiford, who then walks over to Jonah's deserted display. He pulls one of the paintings off the wall and stomps on it, an unintentionally comic childish dance.

CLASSROOM

Audrey enters the figure drawing room. A white-haired **JANITOR** *is sweeping the floor that once held the pile of abandoned art.*

AUDREY: What happened to all the art?

JANITOR: What art?

AUDREY: That stuff that was on the floor.

JANITOR: Oh, the garbage.

AUDREY: Did you see a portrait of me? A–a really beautiful—I–it was right there by your foot.

JANITOR: I chucked everything out back.

CAMPUS
Oblivious to the situation developing across campus, Audrey climbs into an art-filled dumpster and starts digging.

DORM HALLWAY
Uniformed **COPS** *march down the hall, pounding on doors.*

COP #1: JEROME PLATZ!

COP #2: JEROME PLATZ!

DORM BUILDING

Jerome approaches the building from the back. He stops and follows with his eyes a rickety fire escape leading toward the roof.

DORM ROOF

Jerome stands with self-conscious nobility and looks out on the city, like a low-grade Spider-Man. We move in on his tragic countenance and hear his troubled thoughts.

JEROME (V.O.): Audrey, I know you don't care about me, but maybe someday you'll—

He is interrupted by a voice from behind him.

BAKED SOPHOMORE #1 (V.O.): Hey man, don't jump!

Jerome turns around to see the two baked sophomores and their (overweight, dread-locked) female companion sitting in the corner, smoking dope. They laugh at their funny joke. He ignores them and takes a few steps in the other direction. He starts again:

JEROME (V.O.): Audrey, I only hope that someday you'll understand exactly what—

BAKED SOPHOMORE #1: Hey man, don't you live on the fourth floor? You're Vince's roommate, right?

Jerome takes another step away. Can't he please just have one moment of dignity?

BAKED SOPHOMORE #1 (CONT'D): Hey, dude...

Jerome glowers at him. Baked Sophomore #1 just smiles stupidly and proffers the joint.

BAKED SOPHOMORE #1 (CONT'D): Do you partake?

JEROME: No, thank you.

He takes another step.

BAKED SOPHOMORE #1: Hey, tell that jack-off Vince to pay me my thirty-five bucks! Tell him you ran into Whiskey John and he gots to get paid!

Jerome sighs audibly. He moves to the furthest edge of the roof. The Sophomores resume their dopey chatter.

JEROME (V.O.): Maybe when I'm gone, you'll in time come to understand what you and I could have been, what I could have been, if only...

FUTURISTIC ART GALLERY
We find ourselves in 2204 in a THX-1138-*ish art gallery. Two* **ART CRITICS***, dressed in absurd, imagined garb of the future (big red newsboy hats, transparent plastic shirts, very short shorts, platform boots) stand before a wall of Jerome's work, including his self-portrait, the drawing of the big rock, etc. Grouped separately on one side are all the existing drawings and paintings of Audrey including the color portrait.*

FUTURE CRITIC #1: *(their voices have a dreamy futuristic echo)* Most of his work is hollow and derivative, but these portraits of this lovely young girl have an enduring beauty.

FUTURE CRITIC #2: How tragic that he took his life at such a young age.

FUTURE CRITIC #1: Yes, it's a terrible shame. Still, we should be thankful for these few transcendent masterp—

Jerome's reverie is abruptly shattered by loud yelling behind him.

COP #1 (V.O.): GET ON THE GROUND! EAT DIRT!

DORM ROOF
Uniformed cops violently storm the roof and subdue the pot-smokers.

COP #1: KISS THE DIRT, SHIT-HEAD!

BAKED SOPHOMORE #1: Hey, man, I know my righ—

He is shoved face-down into the tar and cuffed. Once the Sophomores are secured, the cops turn to Jerome.

JEROME: Go ahead, do whatever you want to me; I truly don't care if I live or die. Just make sure you tell Audrey that I—OOF!

He is tackled violently from the blind side, pinned face down, and hand-cuffed, with all the resistance of a rag doll.

DORM BUILDING
Down in the street below, there is a swarm of activity—cops, cop cars, students, etc. Jerome is dragged from the building and stuffed in the back seat of the first car. Lonny and Mikey are on hand, trying to keep control of the situation. Kevin screeches up in his unmarked sedan, and Jonah leaps out.

MIKEY: Well there he is.

Jonah heads straight for Lonny.

JONAH: Lonny, I'm sorry...I know I let some personal things get in the way of doing my job, and I just want you to know that—

LONNY: We got him, superstar...All's well that ends well, okay?

He pats him on the back and gives him a we'll–talk–about–this–later look.

MIKEY: Hey Jonah, I hope you don't mind, but I told your wife about all the skanky art-school pussy you been gettin' on the side...

JONAH: You fuckin' asshole, you—

MIKEY: Hey, she was just glad to hear you hadn't gone fag on her!

Jonah grabs him.

MIKEY (CONT'D): Hey, hey, hey—I'm just bustin' your balls!

He puts his arm around Jonah's head.

MIKEY (CONT'D): Good to have you back, douche-bag!

Shilo, Eno and Army-jacket are standing in the crowd outside the dorm.

SHILO: Hey Jonah! *(he looks)* You suck!

Eno spits, narrowly missing Mikey's foot.

ARMY-JACKET: Have a nice death, pig!

Jonah looks genuinely hurt by all this. Mikey goes over and gets in Eno's face.

MIKEY: You want to spit on us again? I'll take you down so fast you got no idea, you fuckin' freak.

LONNY: Mikey! *(Mikey cuts it out and rejoins the other cops)* Let's clear this up and get out of here. *(points toward Jerome)* Kevin, you want to ride with him?

JONAH: Let me do it, Lonny.

Lonny nods and opens the door.

POLICE CAR
Jonah and Jerome sit side-by-side in the back seat. Mikey is driving. The car moves slowly in fits and starts; there is the hint of some sort of hubbub outside. After a long, uncomfortable silence, Jerome finally breaks the ice.

JEROME: I knew there was something weird about you.

Jonah's mouth bends momentarily into a subtle, "look who's talking" smirk.

JONAH: So are you really the guy?

JEROME: *(guileless)* Which guy?

Jonah looks at Jerome, trying to figure him out. He really doesn't seem like much of a murderer.

JONAH: What did you really, you know, think about my...Did you think my paintings were any good at all?

Jerome looks at him. At this point, he can at least afford to let down his defenses and be honest with himself.

JEROME: Yeah, you had something, I guess...There was definitely something there...

JONAH: You think I could have made it as an artist?

JEROME: I don't know about that.

Jonah notices that they've been sitting in one place for awhile.

JONAH: Hey, why aren't we moving?

MIKEY: There's some commotion by the gate...some kids...

The car crawls along. Jerome, still somewhat dazed, looks out the tinted window. There is a teeming crowd by the gate, all screaming for him, straining to get a look, as though he's a movie star arriving at a gala premiere.

JEROME: So what's this all about?

MONTAGE
The following are all shot on video, as though for the evening news:

Professor Sandiford, in his classroom.

PROFESSOR SANDIFORD: Should we judge an artist by what he does in his personal life? If he's an anti-Semite, like T. S. Eliot, or a bully, like Picasso, or, in this case, a murderer, does that mean his art has any less value? I think not!

Broadway Bob, in front of a wall of Jerome's student work (big rock, self-portrait, etc.).

BROADWAY BOB: If I want to have a show of this artist's work, nobody has any right to stop me. I'm fighting for our first amendment rights, here. Either you're with me, or you're a fuckin' Nazi, as far as I'm concerned... *(looks at off-camera director)* Why can't I say that?

Vince, looking tan and successful, sits in his office in front of the poster for "MY ROOMMATE, THE MURDERER," which features a blown-up frame from the Jerome–Audrey kiss. His happy Grandpa sits in a big leather chair behind him.

VINCE: We weren't even sure it was a documentary at first, but then it just sort-of all came together...that's the way I like to work, finding my way as I go along... *(looks over his shoulder)* Isn't that right, Grandpa?

GRANDPA: Tell 'em how much we got for the cable rights!

The Cute Girl from high school, a few years older. She proudly shows off Jerome's drawing of her.

CUTE GIRL: No, I don't think I'd ever sell it...Jerome was always so passionate about his art. It's really unfortunate what happened, but...I mean, I always knew he'd be a famous artist someday...

PRISON

*We are in a clean-looking, no-nonsense modern jail facility, moving down the corridor toward Jerome's cell. The camera enters and wanders casually around the small space. On the wall are various newspaper clippings ("GRISLY ART-SCHOOL SHOCKER," etc), each with the same Weegee-ish police photo of Jerome. We see a stack of identical art magazines with Jerome on the cover, atop an impressive tower of press clippings. The camera finally reaches Jerome, dressed in a paint-spattered orange jumpsuit, standing, brush in hand, before a half-finished painting of Audrey. A friendly-looking **GUARD** taps politely on the bars with his night-stick.*

GUARD: Visiting hours, Jerome.

He opens the door. Jerome sticks out his arms for a per-functory hand-cuffing and follows the guard down the hall.

VISITOR'S ROOM
Waiting in the visitors' room, on the civilian side of bullet-proof glass are Jerome's **LAWYER**, *and his Art Dealer, whom we recognize from Marvin Bushmiller's gallery.*

LAWYER: Look, I just want to do what's best for my client.

ART DEALER: What do you know about what's best? What's best for MY client is to keep him here for as long as possible, followed by a lengthy trial.

LAWYER: I have enough evidence right now to get him out of here...This case shouldn't even go to trial!

The Art Dealer gives him a dirty look. He lowers his voice.

ART DEALER: Where in the fuck did they find you? Jerome needs a lawyer who understands what to do when a situation like this presents itself.

LAWYER: I'm very close to the family.

ART DEALER: That's real nice. Now look, do you know how many paintings I can sell for your client while this is going on? Do you know what an opportunity like this could mean to the career of a young artist?

They notice that Jerome is sitting there, waiting. The Art Dealer picks up the phone.

ART DEALER (CONT'D): Jerome! How's my boy? How's the work coming?

JEROME: Fine.

ART DEALER: You can't believe how many people are calling about you. I had to cut off the waiting list for your paintings.

Jerome is already a little complacent about his success.

JEROME: Great.

LAWYER: *(taking the phone)* Jerome, I just want you to know that everything's going to be fine... *(looks at Art Dealer)* I–it's going to take a little time, but—

ART DEALER: *(grabs phone back)* Did you get a chance to call that guy from *ARTFORUM*? He really wants to talk to you. And did you ever take a minute to look over those papers? If you could sign the yellow one—

Jerome holds the phone away from his ear and turns to the guard.

JEROME: Are these my only visitors?

The guard goes through the steel door to the other side where he ushers away the two visitors.

ART DEALER: Keep your chin up, Jerome; we all love you. I'll call you tonight...

Jerome puts the receiver on the table. He puts his head between his legs and messes up his hair. He turns around and tries to fix himself up in the one-way glass behind him. A familiar voice comes through the receiver.

AUDREY (V.O.): Hi.

He spins around. There she is, all dressed up. She puts her fingertips to the glass, as does Jerome. They stare at each other, overcome.

AUDREY (CONT'D): I–I missed you so much this week...

JEROME: Me too. I–I...

A beautiful, rapturous pause.

AUDREY: Oh Jerome.

At once they erupt into a spontaneous embrace, their lips mashing obliviously on either side of the bulletproof glass. Blissful music swells. Cut to black.

(APPLAUSE)

DANIEL CLOWES: *This story first appeared in EIGHTBALL #7 in 1991. I assumed it would be of no interest to anyone outside of a few of my old art school friends so I kept it very brief, but it turned out that 90% of my readers were either present or former (usually disillusioned & disgruntled) art school students and apparently it struck some kind of a chord. As you will see, aside from a few general "nods," the film bears little more than a passing resemblance in both tone and content to its comic-strip namesake.*

THEY ALL THOUGHT I WAS IN ART SCHOOL TO LEARN THE VARIOUS TECHNIQUES OF SELF-EXPRESSION PURSUANT TO A CAREER IN THE VISUAL ARTS -- AND THAT'S EXACTLY WHAT I WANTED 'EM TO THINK! ACTUALLY, I WAS THERE AS A FREELANCE UNDERCOVER AGENT IN ORDER TO LEARN FIRST HAND THE SHOCKING TRUTH ABOUT THE BIGGEST SCAM OF THE CENTURY!

THE STORY THAT...

BLOWS THE LID OFF A MILLION-DOLLAR RACKET!

ART SCHOOL CONFIDENTIAL

SEE

RICH GUYS WHO DRAW WORSE THAN YOUR SEVEN YEAR-OLD SISTER!

HAS-BEEN FAMOUS-ARTIST PROFESSORS WHO COULDN'T TEACH A DOG TO BARK!

SELF-OBSESSED NEUROTIC ART-GIRLS WHO MAKE THEIR OWN CLOTHES!

THE ART-STUDENT DISGUISE

By D. Clowes, B.F.A.

IN THE OLD DAYS, ART SCHOOLS TAUGHT PRACTICAL TECHNIQUES TO THE EAGER, DEDICATED FEW WHO POSSESSED THE TEMPERAMENT TO KEEP UP WITH A DEMANDING CURRICULUM...

THIS IS A PHOTO AIRBRUSHING CLASS, MISTER -- IF YOU WANT TO DO THAT PICASSO STUFF, GO TO PARIS!

THE TEACHERS ARE NOT THERE TO HELP YOU. MOST OF THEM ARE STILL FREELANCERS AND THE LAST THING THEY WANT IS MORE COMPETITION. THEY ARE THERE BECAUSE THEY NEED A STEADY PAY-CHECK AND THEY HOPE TO SCORE SOME PUSSY!

TODAY, ANYONE WITH A TRUST FUND CAN EXCEL IN CLASSES THAT ARE LITTLE MORE THAN VAGUE PEP-TALKS DESIGNED TO KEEP ENROLLMENT UP BY TRICKING STUDENTS INTO BELIEVING THEY HAVE "POTENTIAL"

I THINK THIS IS NICE... KEEP GOING IN THIS DIRECTION... WHAT DO YOU THINK, CLASS?

NICE.

NICE.

NICE.

KEEP GOING IN THAT DIRECTION

BRAINWASHED SHILLS

"MOM"... COMPLETELY TALENTLESS, RICH HOUSEWIFE WITH TOO MUCH TIME ON HER HANDS.

I'M AFRAID THIS ISN'T COMING OUT THE WAY I WANTED IT TO!

MR. PHANTASY... HE DOES A FRAZETTA-STYLE PAINTING OF A BARBARIAN AS THE SOLUTION TO EVERY ASSIGNMENT!

¿GRUNT?

I-I'M NOT SURE I UNDERSTAND...?

CULTIVATED GRIM, SULLEN DEMEANOR-- JUST LIKE A BARBARIAN!

THE MACHO ART-SADIST... THIS GUY WOULD DRAW HIS GIRLFRIEND IN AN ENDLESS VARIETY OF **HUMILIATING, SEXUALLY SUBMISSIVE POSES** AND THEN MAKE HER COME TO CLASS WITH HIM!

IT COULD ONLY HAPPEN IN ART SCHOOL!

PATHETIC, YET NOT WITHOUT A CERTAIN NEVER-SAY-DIE FIGHTING SPIRIT, THIS DESPERATE FELLOW TRIED TO PASS OFF HIS **TRASHED DORM ROOM** AS A FINAL PROJECT! (AND SUPPOSEDLY ONE OF HIS TEACHERS WENT FOR IT!)

AS AN EXPRESSION OF FRUSTRATION THIS IS NOT WHOLLY INVALID.

RARE IS THE **PRAGMATIST** AMONG ART-SCHOOL PROFESSORS... ONLY VERY OCCASIONALLY DO YOU COME ACROSS SOMEONE WHO IS WILLING TO LEVEL WITH STUDENTS ABOUT THEIR BLEAK PROSPECTS...

ONLY ONE STUDENT OUT OF A HUNDRED WILL FIND WORK IN HIS CHOSEN FIELD. THE REST OF YOU ARE ESSENTIALLY WASTING YOUR TIME LEARNING A USELESS "HOBBY"...

I'LL BE THAT ONE!

FORTUNATELY, TALENT REALLY ISN'T THE ISSUE... FAR MORE IMPORTANT IS THE **GIFT OF GAB!**

DAVID RIVERS TOLD ME AT THE WHITNEY THE OTHER DAY THAT HE FOUND MY WORK TO HAVE TRACES OF LATENT FUTURISM... CERTAINLY THERE IS A CONSCIOUS HOMAGE TO LEGER IN SEVERAL OF MY PIECES BUT THIS ONE OWES MORE TO **BLAH BLAH BLAH**

IF YOU MUST GO TO ART SCHOOL **FOR GOD'S SAKE** MAKE THE MOST OF IT... SELDOM IF EVER AGAIN IN LIFE WILL YOU BE AFFORDED THE CHANCE TO SCRUTINIZE SUCH AN ARRAY OF LOSERS IN AN ENVIRONMENT THAT ACTUALLY ENCOURAGES THEIR MOST PRETENTIOUS INCLINATIONS!

THIS IS MY "SCULPTURE"... I CALL IT "TANGERINE AMOEBA APARTHEID HEARTBEAT IV"

THE OLD TAMPON-IN-A-TEACUP TRICK.

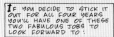

JONAH: PAINTINGS BY D. CLOWE
BFA PRATT INSTITUTE 1984.

JIMMY: BY CHARLES SCHNEIDER. BFA PRATT INSTITUTE 1983. CONTACT: WWW.OUTREGALLERY.COM